the Writer behind the words

Steps to Success in the Writing Life

Dara Girard

ILORI Press
Silver Spring, MD

Copyright © 2005, 2007 Sadé Odubiyi
ISBN 10: 0-9770191-5-2
ISBN 13: 978-0-9770191-5-1

All rights reserved. No part of this publication may be reproduced, stored in a retrieval system, or transmitted in any form or by any means, electronic, mechanical, recording or otherwise, without the prior written permission of the author.

Printed in the United States of America.

Library of Congress Control Number: 2007925222

DISCLAIMER
This book is not intended to provide professional advice and is sold with the understanding that the publisher and the author are not liable for the misconception or misuse of the information provided. The author and ILORI Press shall have neither liability nor responsibility to any person or entity with respect to any loss, damage, or injury caused or alleged to be caused directly or indirectly by the information provided in this book or the use of any products mentioned.

ILORI Press
PO Box 10332
Silver Spring, MD 20914

Cover and Interior Design © 2007 TLC Graphics, *www.TLCGraphics.com*

First Printing 2005
Second Printing 2007 revised

Previously published as *How to Bounce When You Want to Shatter: Steps to Resilience in the Writing Life*

We will be judged
by what we finish,
not by what we start.

ANONYMOUS

Resilience – noun
The ability to recover quickly from illness, change or misfortune; buoyancy

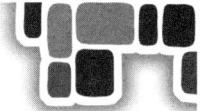

Dedication

*To writers everywhere
who dare to live their dreams.*

Table of Contents

Preface to Revised Edition. ix

Introduction. xi

PART ONE: Assessing Yourself. 1

Search For The Blueprint Of Success 3

Defining Success 5

Six Hard Truths 15

Understanding The Paradox. 19

Seven Traits Of Successful Writers 23

Three Necessary Keys for Resilience 31

Achieve Abundance 35

PART TWO: Surviving the Battlefield 41

Disappointment 43

Discouragement 47

Doubt 61

Depression 65

The Ultimate Dream Killer 69

Getting Started 75

Creative Block 79

Write Anyway 83

Comparison 85

Envy 89

Creative Flood 93

Success 97

PART THREE: Four Steps To Resilience 101

Get Support 103

Relax 105

Know Your Limitations 109

Get a Strategy 113

Success is Your Birthright 117

Recommended Resources 123

Organizations 127

About the Author 131

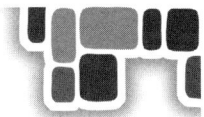

Preface to the Revised Edition

This book started out as a series of articles I planned to put on my website for new authors. I wanted to share with them the pitfalls I had faced as a writer and author. I saw how quickly the joy of creation was crushed by the need for money, the lack of support and obstacles that the writing life throws in the pathway of many. There were many times when I thought I was crazy; that I had no business being a writer.

I had recently parted with an agent, I'd been forced to hire a literary attorney to get me out of a legal position with a publisher and I had been orphaned by two editors leaving in less than two years. I wasn't sure how long my writing career would last. Even my lawyer told me that for someone so newly published I had faced a lot of obstacles. But despite what others may have called misfortune or the plight of the creative person, I never lost my joy of writing.

The Writer Behind the Words

I refused to let the business of publishing destroy my joy of writing. I saw other authors crumble because of a few rejections (it took me thirteen years to get a book published. I started sending out manuscripts when I was twelve) and freelance writers turn in assignments and not get paid (that happened to me and I had to get the law involved). I knew why I was still in the game while others had faded away.

I thought that it was unfair because I wasn't anyone special. I just had one skill they did not: I knew the art of bouncing back.

I wrote this book as a gift to other writers who are discouraged, feel hopeless or useless in a world that can make us—the artist—feel insignificant and invisible. I hope that this revised edition will be a companion to those of you who feel that another day is too painful or that you are alone in your misery.

Isolation is deadly to the spirit, yet, as a writer, a necessary requirement at times. So let this little book be a friend that whispers to you: "You are important and your words are needed."

I dedicate this book to the author of six romances who hasn't sold a story in the past seven years, the mystery writer whose series fails after three books, the mainstream author whose book is remaindered within months of release, the freelancer who has yet to see a check above four hundred dollars, to the beginner who faces another rejection slip in the mail or is struggling through a book and is afraid it will never get published.

I don't profess to be an expert, but I've survived through resilience and I want to show you how. Envy, Doubt, Discouragement — I've faced them all and more. I continue to face them. But they pale in comparison to the beauty and joy of creation and the wonderful gifts it brings.

Introduction

The reason 99% of all stories written are not bought by editors is very simple. Editors never buy manuscripts that are left on the closet shelf at home.
—JOSEPH CAMPBELL

Do you think it's impossible to make a living as a writer because: It's difficult to get published?; the mid-list is shrinking?; fewer people are reading, yet more people are writing?; the market is overcrowded and on a downward spiral?

In spite of these and other dire considerations, there are authors who have bounced back from low sales, sold to publishers without agents, made a handsome income as mid-list writers and reinvented themselves and their careers.

The Writer Behind the Words isn't a "how to write" book. There are plenty of books about how to write a bestseller, improve your grammar, find paying markets, develop your career and so on. This is a book to help you when:

- You're a hundred fifty pages into your book and it stalls. Look at **Creative Blocks**.
- You've received a rejection and can't move forward. Check out **Rejection**.
- A good friend just got a publishing contract and you can see your skin turning green. **Go to Envy**.

You'll also learn what to do with a bad review, how to get your career back on track when it seems to have derailed, foods to help boost your energy, and many other topics important to writers. Someone once said that "our problems aren't our problems; it's our solutions that are the problem." You will learn how to identify solutions that will lead you to success.

I know the traps ahead. When I was an unpublished writer, I dealt with years of rejections, projects that almost got a yes, discouragement, and doubt. As a published author, I have faced poor reviews, being orphaned (by the departure of my editor), breaking up with my agent and a host of other obstacles, but I'm still in the game. I'll reveal how I've kept going in times of adversity, using examples from exercises I've discovered from different sources.

Resilience will help to keep you from becoming an industry statistic. The difference between longevity in publishing and being a "one book wonder" or a "struggling freelancer" is the ability to move forward in spite of setbacks. It's a skill that can be learned. Your dreams are at hand. Forward, march!

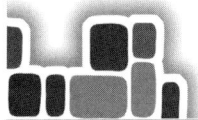

Part One
Assessing Yourself

Search for the Blueprint of Success

Advice to young writers? Always the same advice: learn to trust your own judgment, learn inner independence, learn to trust that time will sort the good from the bad—including your own bad.

DORIS LESSING

Beginning writers are eager for answers. They gobble up articles like: "Ten Secrets to Publication," "Avoid the Slush Pile," and "Don't Get Rejected." Sometimes these articles are as helpful and informative as the staple "Lose Ten Pounds in Ten Days," "Find Your Soul mate in Three Weeks," or "Raise the Perfect Child in A Month." Beginners are full of questions, in search of the elusive key to success. They are full of questions with the hope that the "right" answers will solve everything. They wonder:

Is it best to write during the day or at night?
Should I outline or not?
Should I first send to an editor or agent?
Do I need a critique group or should I enter contests?
Should I write a short story or a novel?
The answer is **yes** to all of the above. Confusing, I know. Some authors will give definite answers to these questions: You must outline. You must have a critique group. You must have a character profile. Thou shalt have no other gods before me...you get the picture. Truthfully, the answers to those questions do not matter because there is no definitive formula.

What does that mean? It means you're in publishing. It means that you'll spend time writing a synopsis and meet a writer who gets a contract without one. It means you'll contact agents and meet a writer who sold directly to a publisher. It means you'll meet writers picked up out of the slush pile and those discovered at conferences. It means you'll meet someone whose first book is a success while yours sinks like an anvil.

There are many different stories on the path to publication and writing success. You will need to create your own. Stop being hungry for a guide or map. Joseph Chilton Pierce said, *To live a creative life, we must lose our fear of being wrong.*

Experiment. If outlines make you lose interest, stop outlining. If you fall asleep at 10:00 PM, don't write at night. This is a business about individuals. Don't try to "do what's right;" do what works for you.

Defining Success

Publication is not necessarily a sign of success.
— WILLIAM SLOANE

Setbacks are a part of any creative endeavor, and you'll find plenty of setbacks in the writing life. You'll lose contests, get nasty reviews, see others succeed before you…and it will hurt.

If you are discouraged to the point that you can't write anymore, I suggest that you stop writing for publication. Write for the joy of it, for personal satisfaction, and not for anyone else. Why? Because publication isn't a cure for anything that ails you and writing doesn't get easier. Stephen King had a cocaine habit *after* he was published, Grace Metalious, the

The Writer Behind the Words

author of *Peyton Place*, drank herself into the ground, and authors still commit suicide.

So if you're hoping that being published will:

Validate you

Make you worthy

Make you happy

Make you successful

Make you attractive

I'm here to tell you it won't. Writing to get "love" (attention, adoration, etc.) is dangerous because not everyone will like your work. They're not supposed to. Even if you sell a million copies, one nasty review will stick in your mind like gum in your hair. You will need to make the act of writing (the creative process) a joy, a cushion for the pain of the business. Someone else will sell more, make more, and have more. It doesn't matter. Your life has nothing to do with them. Enjoy being a creative person, and write.

For many people, external goals never satisfy the inner spirit. Many people get married, have kids, buy a new car, hoping those things will make them happy. They may not. People win the lottery and still end up miserable. If there's something lacking inside you it will still be lacking after publication. You will need to start defining what success means to you. Don't use someone else's definition. Be truthful to your inner desire and need. Don't judge it. Just listen. It's your desire and it's meant to be heard. Get a journal and write about your ideal life. Getting published is great, but go beyond that. Why?

Consider this:

- You could get a couple of articles published and earn a grand total of two hundred dollars for the next five years. Would you consider yourself successful?

- You could get published and get no byline. Is that success?

Defining Success

- You could be published in mass-market paperback instead of hardcover.
- You could have an article published in a magazine no one has ever heard of.
- You could get a six-figure book deal and never publish again and have your book go out of print within a year.

Define success for yourself. Try to make it something that does not depend on others. For example, success could be:

Completing a marketable short story

Developing a synopsis

Writing articles that inform

Editing an anthology

People put a lot of weight on what a "writer" truly is or is supposed to be and in the process they lose themselves trying to achieve a perceived ideal. A writer writes. That's all. Base your success on that foundation. I'm certain it will go beyond just "Getting published."

Goal Versus Mission

Many people confuse goal and mission. Why do you think Mother Teresa said *"More tears are shed over answered prayers than unanswered ones"*? Because many people set and achieve goals only to discover that they are still unhappy. The reason is that goals are fleeting and changeable. They are future events that a person can long for and work towards, but once achieved will become something else. A mission is a lasting motto that carries one through life.

For example, getting published is a goal, being a writer is a mission. Becoming a lead author is a goal, being a diligent, reliable, prolific author is a mission; getting an award is a goal, being an award-winning author is a mission. It's the present moments that give joy. You need to have both goals and a mission as your foundation to carry you through.

Examples of Goals:

Make $100,000 a year
Get my English degree
Become a lead author
Sell 50,000 copies of my book

Example of Missions:

Have a long lasting career
Educate others
Be a good writer
Be healthy

Take the time to create your list of goals and your mission. Remember that a goal has an ending; a mission does not.

The One Secret Every Writer Knows

Most writers are in a state of gloom a good deal of the time; they need perpetual reassurance.
JOHN HALL WHEELOCK

Action is eloquence.
WILLIAM SHAKESPEARE

The secret every full-time writer knows is that *action* is the key to getting what you want. It is the writer's greatest weapon against failure. To achieve this mindset first you have to redefine failure. Failure is not a rejection, a low royalty statement, a book that hits the market and dies or an idea that doesn't work. Failure is stopping your dreams due to circumstance. Failure is receiving one rejection and never writing again.

You may have a fresh start any moment you choose, for this thing we call failure is not the falling down, but the staying down.
MARY PICKFORD

Defining Success

Many new writers tell me how discouraged they are. I understand. I also get discouraged. I tell them to keep going, don't stop, you're great etc. They thank me and go back into the writing world safe in their armor of praise. A few weeks or months later, they write again. They receive a rejection or fail to become a finalist in a contest and they are upset. They bemoan their fate and wail about how unfair the world is and then wait for the expected words of encouragement. But this time I don't provide the same "rah, rah" cheer.

Why? Because in the writing world you have to become your own cheerleader. Most writers fall by the wayside, not due to lack of talent, but due to lack of persistence. Writing is an art and Art (with a capital "A") is bigger than criticism, acceptance, acknowledgement or dismissal.

Art must be created *in spite of*, not because of. Writing because of something (a trend, a contest, an editor etc.) can be a prison to a writer. Your words have only one master— your spirit, which has an unquenchable curiosity and desire to communicate. Well- meaning people will tell you how to write, what to write, when to write or why you should write, but in the end your spirit is your master.

Notice I didn't say *you*, because your conscious self will be too cautious and too clever to write with complete truth. But your spirit is a wild child who sees what you don't and knows what you may not readily admit. It is your free spirit that the world needs. We have enough cautious mask-wearers, we don't need one more in print sounding like everyone else. You must take action.

Action is sending out queries, asking for assignments, writing one more story, jotting down ideas. Action is movement, movement creates energy, energy draws success. Most successful writers have more rejections, setbacks and heartbreaks than writers who have stopped writing. Now that you know the secret, try it for yourself. This can be accomplished by taking small or mini steps.

Mini Steps Towards Action

- Buy a pen and paper.
- Open a file called Writing.
- Develop a ritual. One writer I know has to repeat "I'm brilliant" five times before he starts writing.
- Lower your expectations. Just because a best-selling author writes twenty pages a day doesn't mean you have to. Write a paragraph then congratulate yourself.
- Summarize your idea in a sentence or two.
- Do micro-movements. Read SARK's book (listed in resources section) to find out how.
- Identify writing markets.

Using Your Gifts

Today I looked out the kitchen window of my parents' house and noticed a brown wren. It sat on a railing in their backyard and blended in with the bare trees and dry leaves on the ground. I noticed it, not because it was beautiful, but because it was singing. It sang so loudly that its song echoed through the trees. I stood amazed that something so small could have such a strong voice.

Many of you are just like this wren. You may never be the "bluejay bestseller" or the "eye-catching award-winning cardinal" but your voice will have an impact on those who hear it. So sing — loud and strong.

Preparing for Rain

Always remember that you're good enough as you are to reach your dreams. I know it's hard to believe, especially in a culture that promotes "self-improvement" for every-

Defining Success

thing from physical shape to career choice, but you don't need to change. In spite of all your imperfections, fears, doubts, and worries, you have everything you need to succeed. How do I know this? Because you're here. You're alive and you're no different from others who have traveled this path before you.

Your job is to speak your intentions and to do them. If you truly want to quit, do it now. Why would a book about resilience talk about quitting? Because if you're discouraged by the rain, then the storm is going to kill you.

Some people scoff and think, "Once I'm published everything will be okay. It's worse being unpublished, ignored, having friends laugh at my dreams, having editors dismiss me, and I'm unhappy. A book contract or feature article will at least be an umbrella and then I will be able to deal with the rain."

Yes, publication can be a protection against the rain. I know how hard it is to be unpublished. I was unpublished for years. I know the sting of rejections, the "You're crazy" speech, the dreaded "You've still not published anything?" question, and the "Try something sensible" lecture. Being published allows me to respond to snide comments with a certain wicked delight and conceit that I didn't have before I was published. However, I had confidence *before* I was published. Although publication is an umbrella, it is not a panacea. Can an umbrella keep you safe in a storm? No. What kinds of storms are out there? Consider these:

- After years you finally sell a book to an editor who loves your work. A few months later, the editor leaves and your new editor hates your voice, your main character and you.

- Your agent decides to become a magician.

- An editor kills your article.

- Reviewers sharpen their swords and publicly slice up your work.

The Writer Behind the Words

- "Readers" post nasty reviews online.
- The front cover of your book is lousy.
- The back cover blurb of your book is great; unfortunately it's not what your book is about.
- Sales are low so your publisher drops you.
- You've visited six local bookstores, but can't find your book anywhere.
- You change your name due to low sales and write a different book, which also gets buried in the publishing cemetery.

Still think publication is safe? If you do, I also suspect you'd try holding onto a twig during a tornado.

Publication is nice, but it won't keep you safe. Life happens. How you respond to the obstacles is the key. Many writers have experienced the above impediments and their careers are doing fine. You can do the same, if you're willing to be honest with yourself about what you can handle. How do you deal with setbacks? If you're like most people, you become desperate and either blame life, work harder and grow frustrated, or throw up your hands and give, up saying "I knew I couldn't do it."

Setbacks are not a reflection of you. Later I'll show you how to handle them, but right now you need to face your temperament and see if it matches your goals.

- Do you want to be a writer or to have written?
- Do you want to play it safe or do you mind taking risks?
- Do you live by ultimatums? *"If I don't make it by such and such time, then…"*
- Do you expect to succeed?

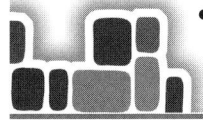

- 12 -

Defining Success

There are no right answers. You know yourself better than anyone else can know you, but it is critical that you know what you're working toward. One thing I have discovered is that people who succeed think in a way that is different from those who don't succeed. People who succeed usually reflect on the future, while those who fail reflect on the past.

If you miss a deadline, do you tell yourself___?

- I'll never succeed because I'm always disorganized OR
- I missed this deadline because I overbooked. Next time I won't do that.

If you get a rejection do you___?

- Shrug your shoulders and submit again OR
- Decide that you're a loser because you always get rejections?

If you submit a manuscript then later learn it was improperly formatted do you___?

- Berate yourself and think of all the other mistakes you've made OR
- Swear, then promise to do better next time?

Do you see the pattern? Winners *always* look forward; they learn from their mistakes, but they do not let past behaviors stop them. There is another trait that separates successful writers from unsuccessful writers — Attitude. I'll give you an example of two writers: Felicity and Malcolm. They have the same world experience, same talent and drive, but different attitudes.

When Felicity gets a rejection, she sees it as a failure. She thinks of all the other authors who haven't received as many rejections as she has. She knows she's not as good as they are, and hates the fact that she's shy. She knows she could never promote and network the way her critique group says she should. She wonders if she has what it takes to make it.

When Malcolm gets a rejection he sighs, is disappointed, and crosses the name of the editor off his list. He knows that marketing is about trial and error and that others have struggled and have ultimately succeeded. He knows that a good product will sell and he doesn't worry that he isn't as outgoing as his friend Randy, who is selling lots of freelance articles. Malcolm knows that there are other writers who are shy, like he is, but who have succeeded. So he keeps on trying.

Felicity and Malcolm are two people with the same problem, but with different attitudes. Work on your attitude or outlook, but don't be mean to yourself. We all make mistakes on occasion. Virginia Woolf sent out her work without her address and a self-addressed stamped envelope for the editor to reply. Remember that all noted writers were once beginners or unknown mid-list writers. Learn to lighten your load and relax. It's hard to run with shackles.

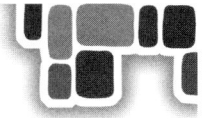

Six Hard Truths

I was going to call this section the six secrets of publishing, because most professional writers don't like to tell new writers about certain realities, but I think it's aptly titled. If you plan to succeed as a writer, you will need to face these six hard truths.

It doesn't get easier.

Writing is an art. As is true with singers or actors, writers are only as good as their last hit. Every book (article, poem) must be created with skill. No book will be a cinch if you strive to grow as a writer. It's a hard thing to face, but your readers will appreciate it.

Someone will always be better than you are.

In this field, someone will always be faster, more prolific, more popular, more creative, or more intelligent. You can't let this distract you. Write anyway. It's okay if you can only write one book a year, or if your imagery isn't stellar or like that of another author. Write.

Talent isn't what you think it is.

I'm sorry to shatter your illusions, but talent in publishing (not to be confused with talented writing) isn't beautiful prose, excellent characterization or any of those other skills you've been working to master. It is about being a wizard with words. Casting spells on people so that they listen to your stories or ideas and pay to read more. In publishing, a writer's talent is measured by one thing: the ability to convince people to *pay* to read her work. So even if someone has the vocabulary of a third grader and ideas as extraordinary as mud… if people buy her work she is seen as talented.

You'll want to quit.

There will come a time when the business of writing won't seem worth it. The pay stinks, the critics are brutal, the readers aren't there, your last book was ignored, or the writing is difficult. You'll want to quit. It's normal. But if your spirit is your guide, you'll discover you can't quit and you'll keep on or start writing again.

You'll get criticism.

Somebody is not going to like your work and will feel the need to tell you about it. It may come to you in the form of a scathing letter, a degrading review or an anonymous hit on

Six Hard Truths

the Internet. It may be public criticism to which you cannot reply (and please don't reply, you'll only look defensive or desperate), or it may be private (which will lead you to fantasize about torching the critic's house). It's part of human nature. We all want to be liked. We want our work to be "loved." That won't always happen. Fortunately, you're not alone. Every writer faces this.

There are no guarantees.

There are no formulas to follow. A good book may not sell. A perfectly written proposal may get rejected. You may follow all the "rules" and see a rule breaker race past you. You may get published then never find a publisher again for years. Focus on writing. Focusing on anything else will make you crazy.

Understanding the Paradox

Paradox - noun
A statement that is seemingly contradictory or opposed to common sense and yet is perhaps true.

I believe in being a cynical optimist or rather an optimistic cynic because it's easier to live that way. Writers who are pervasive pessimists are unhappy no matter what good fortune comes to them, and writers who are naively optimistic are easily crushed and disappear after a couple years. Neither lasts long in publishing. Pessimists are stopped because they build up many reasons to fail and then usually do. Optimists don't make it because they expect everything to work out and never prepare for (or even consider) the possibility of disappointments. When setbacks come, they think that it's their fault or it blindsides them and they sink in despair.

If you are to survive, you will need to believe in success and abundance, that your career is within reach and that you can make a living as a writer. But you will also need to realize that it may be a struggle at first.

The writing life has many contradictions. If you get nothing else from this book, please remember what Admiral Stockdale said in Jim Collins' bestselling business book *Good to Great*:

> *You must never confuse faith that you will prevail in the end— which you can never afford to lose—with the discipline to confront the most brutal facts of your current reality, whatever they might be.*

Admiral Stockdale should know. He survived a POW camp and saw "the optimists" die of broken hearts. Optimists in the writing world usually make career plans saying "By this age I will be here" (What happens if you're not?) Or they determine that "I will make this much money by this time" (what if your career has a slow start?) "If I don't win or final in this contest, then I'll quit" (Why not quit now?) Some optimists employ the annoying practice of "positive thinking," believing that their thoughts will alter their destiny. While I do believe that our minds are our most powerful tool, I find no harm in facing reality.

If you're worried that your manuscript may get lost in the mail, print out a second copy just in case. If you're afraid that your writing is not good enough, then take the time to learn how to make it better. Our thoughts, both good and bad, are a gauge of our present reality. If you can't write well, "positive thinking" won't change that. However, you can think positively as you write (the difference is passivity versus action). Don't ignore your feelings by trying to "think positive." When I drive somewhere I hope to get there in one piece without incident; however, I still put on my seatbelt.

The Stockdale Paradox

Retain faith that you will prevail in the end, regardless of the difficulties and at the same time confront the most brutal facts of your current reality, whatever they may be.

Seven Traits of Successful Writers

Now that you understand the paradox, you can go to the next step. Here are seven traits of successful authors that can help you on your road to resilience.

Resistance to fear, mastery of fear—not the absence of fear.
MARK TWAIN

Everyone has talent. What is rare is the courage to follow that talent to the dark place where it leads.
ERICA JONG

Courage

It takes a quiet arrogance to be a creative person, to create something that no one really needs and then demand compensation. As a writer your courage will be tested. You will need courage to hold your head high when a book has low sales, fails to find a publisher or is publicly dismissed or criticized. You will need courage to face the outside when: people laugh at your efforts or dismiss them, readers pan an article, or a poem is called "too pretentious." Making decisions also takes courage. You may have to decide whether to stay with an agent or leave, or to end a collaboration that has turned sour although it is financially fruitful.

At times, fear will limit your options; you must have the courage to expand those options. You can't deny the presence of fear, doubt, or anxiety because they never leave. They will be there as you type your manuscript, as you place it in an envelope and as you write your query. All writers feel it; don't let it paralyze you. Have the courage to write through it.

Ways to Improve Your Courage

- Try a foreign dish.
- Fail fast! Many people are terrified of getting a rejection. So get one and get it over with.
- Write your book, poem or article badly. It takes courage to face that you're imperfect.
- Read your work aloud.
- Write in a style you consider difficult and then treat yourself for trying.

Teachability

Man can learn nothing except by going from the known to the unknown.
CLAUDE BERNARD

Competence can be a killer of excellence. Many writing careers get buried because the writer becomes complacent. They have reached the goal of publication and no longer strive to be the best at what they do. They fall into familiar plot twists, language, characters or subjects. It's safe (they get paid and have a readership), but this tendency puts most writers in a rut. Successful writers are always willing to learn. They aren't stuck in their ways and can reinvent themselves when the time is right. Perfect examples are Dean Koontz, who went from writing four small books a year to writing big mainstream novels; Jennifer Crusie, who jumped out of category romances into women's fiction; and Sandra Brown, who also left category romance to write suspense novels. No matter how long you have been writing, you don't know everything. You will need to keep your mind open.

Ways to Improve Your Teachability

- Read a book about the writing craft or motivational books.
- Try something new. If you write articles, try poetry; if you write books, try short stories.
- Learn the skills to become a good listener.
- Read something out of your area of expertise.
- Seek advice from a trusted writing buddy.

Persistence

Half the failures of this world arise from pulling ones horse as he is leaping.
AUGUSTUS HARE

In spite of setbacks and obstacles, successful writers continue to write. They don't quit. They fall down, but get up again no matter how hard the blow. Many of us feel helpless and out of control when something unexpected happens. We then spend time blaming people or circumstance. Most people get stuck at this stage and wallow in "what could have been."

Successful writers, on the other hand, move past this stage and come up with a new strategy. Persistence is the trait of all great artists. You'll need to develop yours.

Ways To Improve Your Persistence

- Make your plans public. If you're going to write an article, have a friend keep tabs on you. Make yourself accountable.

- Measure your commitment to your goal. How much does it mean to you? What will happen if you don't reach it?

- Write down your mission statement. Keep it somewhere so you can see it.

- Listen to music you love, especially warrior music (themes from movies where a character overcame obstacles or anything that inspires you, whether it be a rowdy country song, rock, or a gospel tune).

- Come up with alternative plans to reach the same goal.

- Call someone for a pep talk or a strategy session.

- Create a chant. "I'm a lean, mean writing machine." "When I write, the world is at my mercy."

Vision

The future belongs to those who see possibilities before they become obvious.
John Sculley

We are all called to serve in one way or another. Successful writers know their purpose is to serve the world through writing. I encourage you to come up with your life mission statement. Do you want to entertain children? Instruct, heal, or encourage people? Your words will be a gift to the world, know what you want them to do.

Seven Traits of Successful Writers

Ways to Improve Your Vision

- Dream big dreams! The kind that make your heart race. The kind that you're a little afraid might come true. (Don't forget to write them down.)
- Identify your audience. You can't properly serve people you don't understand. Have someone in mind when you're writing, even if it's you.
- Envision what kind of book has your name on it. What does it look like? Is it hardcover or paperback? Sketch out an idea.
- Create a brilliant review for your book.
- Create letters to the editor that applaud your article.
- Create a list of magazines –in which you would like to see your byline.
- Write a tale, or imagine how your work will affect people. Do you see an entirely different storytelling style? A hybrid genre?
- Go to a bookstore and imagine seeing your books there on the shelves.
- Envision your life in five years, then ten. Write down what you're doing, where you're living, and how you go about your day-to-day activities.

Grace

Conceit spoils the finest genius. There is not much danger that real talent or goodness will be overlooked long; even if it is the consciousness of possessing and using it well should satisfy one, and the great charm of all power is modesty.
LOUISA MAY ALCOTT

Many of the top writers don't gossip about the industry or other writers. They don't grumble online or gripe about their woes to anyone who will listen. They don't go to conferences to have a whinefest (writers are great whiners). I won't say they are model citizens, but they are generous with their time and knowledge (yes, I know there are exceptions, but you don't want to be one of those, I hope). These writers are humble about their gifts, don't talk about their competition in unflattering terms and are respected in the field.

Ways to Improve Your Grace

- Offer advice to someone who is struggling.
- Give praise.
- Find out the names of people you work with, the name of the editor's assistant, your postal carrier. Acknowledge them from time to time.
- Send gifts for no reason.
- Limit the time you spend online in chat rooms, blogs, message boards or loops. It's very easy to slip into gossip.

Clarity

*If you despise your readers,
they will probably despise you.*
ANDREW GREELEY

Great writers don't try to impress their readers with large vocabularies or grand ideas. They write to be understood, to instruct or entertain—nothing more. Don't play it safe, say what you mean; let your words shine.

Ways to Improve Your Clarity

- Use both short and long sentences.
- Read books on craft (e.g., *The Elements of Style* by Strunk and White)

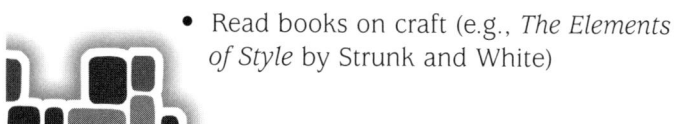

Seven Traits of Successful Writers

- Identify your audience. Keep them in mind as you write. Writing for teenagers is different from writing for middle-aged housewives or immigrant students.
- Measure the readability of your prose. You can find tools for this in Microsoft Word and other resources. Remember most successful writers write at the 6th grade level or below.

Faith

*Creativity comes from trust. Trust your instincts.
And never hope more than you work.*
RITA MAE BROWN

*By listening to the creator within, we
are led to our right path.*
JULIA CAMERON

Many successful writers have a spiritual connection, not necessarily a religious one. They are in tune with themselves and their place in the universe. They believe that writing is what they are meant to do and have faith that things will turn out well. Faith is sometimes seen as a dirty word or merely a religious one. Don't make this mistake. Faith is the foundation of dreams realized. When all looks bleak, faith is your sunshine. When the statistics are against you, faith makes them meaningless. Will your faith get shaken? Probably. Is that bad? No. Just don't let the doubts last. Constantly focus your energy on the future that you want, not the future that you don't want. If you don't want to stay broke, don't study why writers struggle or get low pay. Study the rich ones and model them.

If you don't want to be an obscure author, don't read about the lives of authors who died in poverty and had their work discovered after their death. Study those who were successful in their own time. **Study success.** Surround yourself with people and things that propel you forward. Once you are a financial success, then you can worry about the plight of the lowly author and provide help.

Ways to Improve Your Faith

- Learn to listen to your gut, instincts, or whatever you wish to call it.
- Learn to say "no" to things that aren't part of your plan. The world will not crash and burn if you tell your sister you can't baby-sit or that you can't help your neighbor with his taxes this year.
- Write about anything for fifteen minutes without stopping.
- Write affirmations (more on this later) and say them every day.

Three Necessary Keys for Resilience

It is the constant and determined effort that breaks down all resistance, sweeps away all obstacles.

CLAUDE M. BRISTOL

There are three traits that can determine whether you will be successful with resilience: passion, focus and initiative.

Passion

Passion is a great equalizer. Success doesn't depend on intelligence, degrees or talent. Success depends on passion. All the great figures in history had a burning passion and achieved amazing things. You can too. Keep the fire of desire burning in your heart and you'll find the solutions to all obstacles. Passion will delete the word "impossible." Enthusiasm will make every day exciting. Get in touch with what makes you angry, happy or miserable. Experience these feeling and come alive again.

When you live with passion, your life will expand in ways you could never dream of.

Focus

The secret of success is constancy of purpose.
BENJAMIN DISRAELI

Put your energy into developing your strengths. Too many people spend their time trying to become perfect. They put their focus on trying to fix their procrastination or nasty temper or bad habits instead of focusing on what they want. The sun is a huge source of light and energy; the laser is much smaller, yet a laser can do more damage. The reason is focus. Focused energy is very powerful.

You don't need to be perfect to achieve your goal. You're not a car or a machine that needs all the kinks smoothed out in order to work properly. You're a human with unlimited potential. Focus on your strengths and how they can serve your purpose.

Discover what your career is about (or what you want it to be about). Try to limit it to one thing. Is it about entertainment? Enlightenment? Healing? What is your core theme? All writers have a core theme that runs through their work, both fiction and non-fiction, no matter the format. Find yours. It will keep you from being swayed from your mission.

Initiative

Don't wait for the wind; start paddling the boat. Many writers like to wait for inspiration. Reach out and grab it or, better yet,

Three Necessary Keys for Resilience

do without it. Write, write, write. Don't wait for the right moment, right idea or the right equipment. Get started. As I said earlier, action is the key to success.

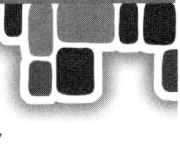

Don't confuse praise with self-worth. Some people will love your work, award it and congratulate you. Others will strike it down and call you names: hack, amateur, semi-literate twit. Accept the words that build up your spirit and ignore the rest.

Expect success and work towards it. Make your attitude your ally. You don't have to "think positive" but you do need to believe that you are worthy of a successful, abundant, and joyful life. What you think will make your journey difficult or easy. If you were told that tomorrow you would be greeted with a huge bouquet, wouldn't you wake up with joy? But if you were told that you would be greeted by a punch in the nose, wouldn't you wake up with dread? Neither incident may happen but what you *think* will happen is key to how you will face the next day. So tell yourself wonderful things. Since you're on this journey, you might as well enjoy it.

Achieve Abundance

> To be nobody but yourself in a world which is doing its best, night and day, to make you everybody else—means to fight the hardest battle which any human being can fight and never stop fighting.
>
> E.E. CUMMINGS

You can succeed as you are with all your doubts and fears. But there are thoughts that will hinder your progress and may even sabotage your dreams. Many people live with beliefs that depress them and limit their freedom from fear. Here are some thoughts to throw away:

Life is about suffering
Only the strong survive
You have to struggle to get what you want
It's a dog eat dog world
You must sacrifice everything to reach your dreams
Poverty is the price an artist pays for freedom
It's selfish to want to be rich
God doesn't like money
Only certain people are blessed
Some people are lucky and I'm not one of them

These thoughts are based on a concept of "scarcity thinking." Scarcity thinking is the belief that there is only a limited amount of money, ideas, time, energy, and whatever to go around. Many people live as though lacking something is a part of life. This type of thinking creates a competitive and unhealthy atmosphere and makes the spirit wither. That is why, when people suffer a disappointment or setback, they become angry at those who succeed. They become bitter seeing others achieve what they believe should be theirs. Their hearts ache when they see someone win an award, reach a bestseller's list, or make other achievements because they think it should have been them.

People can't help feeling this way. We are raised in a very competitive society and we are programmed to think that for someone to win others must lose. That is true in the limited world, but in the world of abundance that is not true. Everyone wins. They just have to wait their turn. There are money, ideas, and time enough for you, if you stop trying to horde them, and try instead to live with peace.

Remove thoughts of scarcity from your mind and move free into the world of abundance. There is plenty to go around. The universe has abundant riches waiting for you to tap into. Open your mind to the possibility of a life where you can write and make a living for yourself and your family. A life where you can make a living doing what you love. It can be a frightening thought to believe that you can work towards your dreams and see them come true. Have the courage to try.

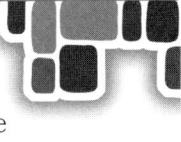

Finding your Spiritual Guide

False beliefs are the shadows that keep people safe and in the dark. An affirmation is a light in that darkness. It is a statement of what you want to be true now. *I want to be a writer* is not an affirmation, *I am a writer* is. You may balk at what I'm saying and your inner critic may rise up and mock you. Good. Listen to it. You have to face it in order to defeat it.

Pay attention to the thoughts that come to the surface. Are they familiar ones that have held you back before? What voices of "reality" keep you from joy? A number of our fears start with our religious upbringing that has taught us about a God (if you are not religious you can replace the term God with universe or energy) that is cold and unfeeling and wants us to suffer for the ultimate good. I had a hard time believing in such a being. I didn't think God would give me a desire to write then punish me for it. If you have a desire to create, that is how you are to serve the world. You are not a mistake.

God is the ultimate artist. Just look at the world around you, the various languages, music, and colors. God respects and delights in your gifts. I suggest that you create the following two lists. List ten characteristics of the God of your past, the vengeful angry God that you grew up with. The one you were taught to fear. The one you believe will never let you live your dream because you're not good enough. The one that thinks there is honor in poverty, the one that would never support you being an artist. Write down ten of his (her/its) characteristics. Next write ten attributes of God as you would like him/her/it to be. Kind, supportive, loving, generous with money and ideas.

Next, look at both lists. There you will see your past and future. Release the God of your past and grasp the hand of the God of your future. Get to know that God and make him (her/it) your spiritual leader and guide. Believe in a universal spirit that wants you to be happy.

> "Genius begins great works; labour alone finishes them."
> JOUBERT

Secret Truths

No one has to fail so that you can succeed. As stated before, many people believe that the world is about survival of the fittest. That is not so. You do not have to be an aggressive barbarian in order to get what you want. You can be generous and kind and still succeed. Sometimes it's the thoughts of society that stop us, but other times it is our own inner truths.

Create a list of reasons why you can't succeed as a writer. **I can't succeed because...**

I'm not smart

I have poor grammar

I don't have time

I have a family to support

I'm too conservative to be a real artist

I'm disorganized

I'm not bold enough

I don't like to take risks

I'll probably fail

Come up with your own reason(s), then identify ones that sound like a past discourager (a parent, teacher, sibling, current myth) and release them. Identify the ones that reveal your own hidden fears. Acknowledge then release them. You may not be able to identify where some of these reasons come from. That doesn't matter. Just acknowledge them, then release them.

Yes, I know it sounds corny, especially when the car won't start, you've had low scores on every contest you've entered, you've reached a certain birthday or you haven't managed to sell any writing in three years. I know it may sound silly, but as Napoleon Hill said, what the mind believes it can achieve.

One writer I know regularly told herself "I am a multi-published author" for the six years she was unpublished, and today she has five books on the market and is under contract for two more. So create a statement of power—an affirmation—for your life.

Remember that an affirmation is a "now" statement:

I deserve success

All my needs are met

I am rich

I make $___ a week

I have an audience that appreciates my work

I write successfully in three genres

Now that you have faced yourself, let's move to the battlefield.

Part Two
Surviving the Battlefield

Disappointment

A fellow author, whom I'll call Patricia, recently faced a hard lesson in disappointment. She'd signed a second two-book contract with her publisher and had sent in her first book under the new contract. She was excited, and prepared her promotion schedule for the next year as she began working on her fourth book.

A few months later, she received notice that her editor did not like the third book and was reneging on the contract. She was let go without an explanation. No new book, no check—nothing. The disappointment was crushing. All her plans, all her excitement—dashed. Someone else may have crumbled, but Patricia didn't.

She continued to promote her first two published books and sent out queries on her third book. At a writer's conference she met an editor and convinced her to look at her manuscript. The editor agreed. Months later that editor offered Patricia a two-book contract.

That is what resilience is about. Patricia could have let the disappointment stop her, but she didn't wallow in it. She shared her pain with fellow authors and kept sending out queries. She wouldn't let one person's judgment stop her from her dream and her readers are thankful.

Disappointment sneaks up on you. Life is fine then WHAM! A book doesn't sell-through well, a story is pulled, an imprint closes or a magazine goes out of business before your article can get printed. It's okay to feel let down. It's okay to be upset, but move on. Patricia could have gotten angry and held a grudge against the editor. She could have whined about how this editor had stopped her career, but she didn't. She kept going.

Steps to Dealing with Disappointment

Share the disappointment like Patricia did. Don't keep your feelings bottled up, there's no need to feel ashamed. A setback is not a reflection of your self-worth or your talent. Another author had an editor reject her work because she liked "light, funny stories" and found the author's work "too dark." I had an agent who lost complete faith in one of my books and refused to send it out. It was devastating, but I decided to move forward.

Keep sending out. Come up with a new strategy. Inventors face lots of disappointment. When an experiment doesn't work, they try a new way and keep on trying.

If you're in the mood, try to find a lesson in the disappointment. This is not the time for blame; think of it as a career autopsy. What went wrong? Patricia discovered that her old publisher wasn't the right place for her work. Instead of trying to send them new proposals (and likely stalling her career), she moved on and found a supportive editor and new publisher who will help grow her career. She learned from her disappointment that she was in the wrong jungle.

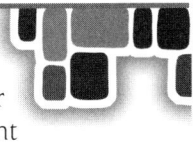

Extra

How to Perform a Career Autopsy

Take responsibility. If your agent suggested a change that you made and the book still didn't sell, don't blame the agent. You made the decision to change. Why? How may that have influenced things?

Analyze your decisions and the market. Were you trying to follow a trend? Is there a bad market climate? Were you marketing to the wrong audience? Is your productivity not what it could be?

Are you in the wrong writing field (fiction versus nonfiction)? Genre (mystery versus fantasy)? Many authors try to write what is popular and fail miserably because that is not their strength. Also, what you like to read may not be your voice. I like to read dark mysteries, but my books always tend to have humor in them. If I tried to write another way, I wouldn't succeed.

Identify harmful habits. Do you miss deadlines? Make sloppy edits? Have slim plots or dull characters?

Discouragement

Discouragement comes in many forms. Rejections, poor reviews and the doom and gloom comments of a "Wet Blanket" can ruin a great day. It takes a lot of courage to face them and keep moving forward, but with the right knowledge you can.

Rejection

*I discovered that rejections are not altogether a bad thing.
They teach a writer to rely on his own judgment
and to say in his heart of hearts, 'To hell with you.'*
SAUL BELLOW

First you feel as though you're dying. It doesn't matter how: whether you were shot through the heart, knifed through the gut, or poisoned. All you know is that your life will soon end and you don't care. You stand in front of your mailbox with your returned manuscript and a letter from the editor feeling completely alone in your grief and sense of failure.

Rejection hurts, whether it is a cold form letter or an encouraging "Try again." Rejections can make you begin to question yourself.

Who am I to write?

What the heck am I doing?

I'm an idiot to try this.

If I'm so great why doesn't anyone else think so?

"Don't take it personally" people say, but it feels personal.
I mean, the letter was addressed to me!

Rejections stinks. I know. I've received over two hundred rejections in my career and still get some in the mail and online. However, it also means that I'm working, creating, and producing. Rejection is a part of life and definitely part of the writer's world. Don't give it power.

You reject things every day. You turn on the TV and flip through the channels. You go to a restaurant and skim through the menu until you see what you want. You go into the bookstore and pass hundreds of books until you find one you think you will like. Why did you pass the others? Because they are unworthy or because they are poorly written? No. You passed them because you have distinct tastes. So do agents and editors. They are people just like you and me.

What does that mean? It means you're in the sales business and you have to convince people to buy a product. Not everyone will buy. Be ready to move on. It's part of the process. It stings, it burns, it wounds, but you'll heal. It's an opinion, not a life sentence. When an editor or agent says, "Doesn't fit our present needs" or "Not enthusiastic enough about this" they are not saying: "You are now sentenced to be unpublished for the rest of your life. Why are you trying to write? Why

Discouragement

are you wasting my time? Quit now before you embarrass yourself and everyone who knows you." They are not laughing evilly as they toss your manuscript back to you. It's basically an "I'm not interested" and that's it. Keep writing; keep sending out.

You never know what will make a sale. The fantastic story you wrote about life and death colliding may be turned down while your so-so article on ants infesting a picnic will get picked up. It's not personal—it feels like it, but it's not. They don't even know you, and frankly they don't care. Editors and agents have an agenda. Sometimes you're not on it; write anyway. Send out anyway.

> *I quickly learned that if I kept at it and plowed right through the rejections I would eventually get somebody to buy my wares.*
> CHARLES SCHWAB

Ah, but what about those nasty notes? The ones where the editor or agent takes the time to tell you that you need writing classes, that you should stop writing and have more babies (advice given to Danielle Steel) or that your writing is "too slight" (told to Mary Higgins Clark). Be wary of such advice. Remember it's just an opinion. Unless there's a common thread in all your rejections, it doesn't mean anything. One editor will say they love your hero, but hate your plot; another will say they love your plot, but hate your hero. That criticism won't help you. So trust your gut. The publishing industry is a very subjective field. Only you know the value of your manuscript.

Some editors and agents are jaded readers cocooned in their New York sensibilities and think in terms of salability rather than what readers will enjoy. They will reject a small town premise because they believe it will be uninteresting or because another book set in a small town didn't sell well and they think yours won't sell well either. Editors and agents aren't bad people, just recognize that their job is to make money for their companies, not to foster your writing dreams.

Your response to rejection will influence your career. If you try to avoid it, you could stop sending out or stay safe by sending to low paying markets. If you don't risk rejection, you won't have to face the lingering doubt that maybe you're not good enough. Unfortunately, however, you'll have made a career-killing decision, all on the basis of an overworked agent or editor who has to make a split decision on whether she thinks you'll sell or not.

You will dislike this individual. You will wish that she break out in spots, lose all her teeth, and then one day see your book on the *New York Times* bestseller's list and cry bitter tears for having misjudged you. This is perfectly understandable. But let it go. Business is business. Don't threaten suicide or send foul letters. It won't change her mind and may influence others not to work with you. The publishing industry is small. Remember, editors and agents have rejected wonderful works in the past and will continue to do so.

How to Recover from a Rejection

Remember what Barbara Kingsolver said: *This manuscript of yours that has just come back from another editor is a precious package. Don't consider it rejected. Consider that you've addressed it 'To the editor who can appreciate my work' and it has simply come back stamped 'Not at this address'. Just keep looking for the right address.*

- Use it as a reminder that you're working. Salespeople (no matter what field) expect to hear "No" because they know each "No" brings them closer to a "Yes." A rejection is not a brick wall, it's just a bump in the road. Keep moving forward.

- Picture yourself succeeding. Imagine this rejection as a story you'll use in your acceptance speech as you're awarded a major prize.

- Have another envelope ready to ship out right away so that you have hope again.

Discouragement

- Talk to a friend.
- Have a rejection party. Celebrate it. Buy a small cake or trinket so that rejection won't be something to dread.
- Reward yourself. Come up with a quota. If you get ten rejections, then you get to go to a movie. If you get twenty, you get to buy something you want. Have a trusted friend in on the game and come up with a point system.
- Save them for your taxes. You can use them as proof that you are a writer.
- Read books about rejected authors who have succeeded.
- Recognize that sometimes the rejection is saving you from public humiliation. Your work may not be ready yet. Keep writing; keep working on your craft.

Bad Reviews

The lot of critics is to be remembered for what they failed to understand.
GEORGE MOORE

It's going to happen to you. Somebody with the intelligence of a pimple, somewhere is going to criticize your work; not constructively, mind you, but with the sole intent of demolishing your work and making themselves feel witty. You'll have to remember that the basis of wit is caustic comments. Wit is a game of words that should not be confused with wisdom.

Reviews are the bane of a writer's existence. Get a good one and you'll feel great and scared. Get a bad one and you'll feel awful and scared. They are an unfortunate necessity but have no real guidelines. A writer must remember that reviewers have a motive — To be read and to keep their jobs. They want people to read them, not necessarily your book. They are writers with hidden agendas.

Some are kind; some are cruel. But they don't count, readers do. Stephen King and other top writers still get bad reviews and it hasn't hurt their careers (although undoubtedly their feelings were hurt). Stephanie Bond received a one star review in a major romance magazine for her book and that book ended up becoming one of her most popular books due to the one component the reviewer found so offensive. Lori Foster is a bestselling author of over sixty books and still gets nasty reviews.

Keep writing. Read reviews if you must, otherwise ignore them and continue to create.

A good writer is not, per se, a good book critic.
No more than a good drunk is automatically a good bartender.
JIM BISHOP

What to do With a Bad Review

- Send a thank you to the reviewer (at least they read the book and it might freak them out).

- Remember that most people read reviews to find out about the book not the reviewer's opinion.

- Highlight the "money words" then send the review to your editor. Some poor reviews have great quotes you can use.

- Review the reviewer. Is the review well written? Does it get the gist of your story right? Is it littered with personal attacks and unnecessary opinions? Angry readers blasted one reviewer in my local paper because her review of a non-fiction book was poorly done. She had misinterpreted the intention of the writer and misrepresented what the book was about. The paper had to apologize and the author got much needed publicity.

Discouragement

- Read the poor reviews of books you have enjoyed. It helps to put reviews into perspective.
- Flush it down the toilet or get your dog to pee on it.
- Cry with a friend.
- Find out what the reviewer disliked and then do that some more. That is what will make your work unique. Jean Cocteau said: *Listen carefully to first criticisms of your work. Note just what it is about your work that the critics don't like—then cultivate it. That's the part of your work that's individual and worth keeping.*
- STOP READING THEM

The Wet Blanket

A successful man is one who can lay a firm foundation with the bricks that others throw at him.

DAVID BRINKLEY

Some people mistakenly believe that rejection and bad reviews are the ultimate discouragement. They are not. For writers (or any creative artist) the Wet Blanket is one of the most dangerous of all the discouragers because they mask themselves as friends.

As you pursue your dream, you will discover that not everyone will cheer for you. Some will give you reasons why you will fail. They will make statements like, "This is good, but it's no (fill in successful author's name)." "Twenty-five dollars for an article? You certainly couldn't live on that." "Do you know how competitive the market is?" "Hey I just saw that you got one star on Amazon. Ouch! I'd hate to be you." "Another rejection? Man, maybe you should give up this writing thing."

They will tell you about how impossible it is to succeed as a writer. You must ignore them. Wet Blankets are usually blocked creatives or people who are fearful of change. Seeing

The Writer Behind the Words

you go after your dream may shine a light on the dreams they let die. Some will be relentless in their comments, you will have to distance yourself from them or end the acquaintance. With family members you can instruct them that they can talk about anything *but* your writing career. Set boundaries.

Also be careful of critique groups, workshops, and writing instructors. Great ones will inspire and encourage you and keep you moving forward. Bad ones can stop you forever. One writer stopped writing because a teacher read his story aloud in class then called it an example of how a story shouldn't be written. Another up-and-coming writer stopped her career because a boyfriend felt threatened by how much time her writing took away from him.

Group dynamics can create a group mentality. A teacher may only applaud a certain type of writing style and hold it up as an example for the other writers in the group to emulate. A critique group may belittle your story because it doesn't stay within the accepted structure of a certain genre. Don't let your creativity be stifled by someone else's limited vision.

Remember, there will be people who will not want to see you succeed. It's very important that you recognize these dream killers and stay away from them.

Dealing With a Wet Blanket

- Protect your joy. If you're excited about something, don't share it with someone you know won't be happy for you. Keep some secrets. Don't tell everyone what you're up to. Trust only a few with your dreams.

- Recognize them. Identify the Wet Blankets in your life and write a letter to them. You don't have to mail it.

- Create a "no talk" topic. If you are with a Wet Blanket have a conversation limit.

- Remember the source. Unless they are living the life you want to lead or are sincerely invested in your success, their comments aren't helpful.

- Create distance. Change is difficult for many people. They would have a hard time if you lost weight or got a high paying job so let them deal with their feelings without dumping on you.

- Make new friends. Join groups or find another person who is a constant support and turn to him when the going gets tough.

Kidders

Next to Wet Blankets are Kidders. Those who make harsh comments then pretend to soften the blow by saying "Just kidding" or "Just joking."

This scene is so boring I could use it as a barbiturate. Just kidding!

You didn't even go to college. How could you write anything someone would read? Just kidding!

You really pump out those books like a true hack. Just joking!

You write like a second grader. Just joking.

The best way to combat these crude attacks on your ego is to:

- Not laugh. Many of us try to shrug it off and see the humor for fear of being deemed "too sensitive." Kidding is not funny. Don't laugh at what's not humorous and the person will get the message.

- Be careful who you share your dreams and good news with. Some people will not take the hint that their kidding is painful, so don't allow them to use you as a target.

- Realize that they're scared. A lot of humor comes from pain. It's their pain and you don't need to soothe it.

Bad Agents and Editors

Over the past several years, I've met enough agents and editors to know that they can be wonderful people and that to have them in your corner is a great asset to your career. Unfortunately, not all agents and editors are good. Some are downright cruel and very harmful to a writer's career and self-esteem. It doesn't matter why they behave as they do (they're going through a hard time; they're failed writers, etc.). The only solution is to get away from them.

Because publication depends so much on others, many writers put their lives in the hands of agents and editors and don't watch their careers. Don't do this. Not everyone has your best interests in mind. This field is crawling with scam artists. Your best defense is to make all your business relationships peer relationships or partnerships, rather than parent/child relationships.

How to Spot a Bad Agent

- Typos in the correspondence.

- Promises to make you a "star." Everyone likes to get his ego stroked, scam artists know this.

- Doesn't submit your work.

- Sends you form rejection letters. (These are the generic "Dear Writer" letters that publishers send out. Unscrupulous agents just copy them and send them to clients to show that they're "working").

- Blames you (or your project) for not selling. Agents must be passionate about your work. Once they lose faith, your relationship is over.

- Charges a fee for anything. Writers NEVER need to pay agents. Agents get their money once they sell the book. It can be agreed that the cost of printing and shipping can come from the

Discouragement

first advance check or an agreed upon amount prior to signing the contract. Don't pay an upfront fee for the cost of doing business.

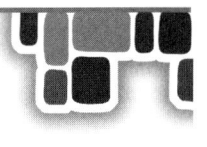

- Won't address key questions. You should know your agent's marketing plan for your work. What happens when they get a "No?" How many times will they submit a project?

- Won't return your calls or emails.

When searching for an agent, make sure to research their credentials, have an idea of what you want for your career (don't let anyone make that decision for you), and make sure they have a verifiable track record. Anyone can say they've sold a book to the big publishers. Get proof. Even when you get a good agent you still need to be your own best advocate.

Bad editors are similar to bad agents, except they get a salary so they can afford to be cruel.

How to Spot a Bad Editor

- Doesn't communicate. Doesn't return phone calls, faxes, emails etc…

- Makes you feel insignificant. Continually reminds you that you're not her only author.

- Tries to change your writing style.

- Puts you down by comparing you to his bestselling authors or other writers for the magazine.

- Never offers you any encouragement. Every writer deserves a "good job" every once in a while.

- Doesn't read your manuscript, just sends it into production.

- Never sends you your money on time.

There are other discouragers out there that may strike. When they do, try the following activities.

What to do When You're Discouraged

- Clean out the clutter. Get rid of clothes you don't wear anymore, remove plates or pots you never use, toss out socks with holes or shoes that have no soles. Wear clothing that makes you feel good; use items that make you feel proud.
- Exercise.
- Get a hug. Sounds silly, but touch really can help. If you can get more than a hug, great. (Come on, don't be a prude).
- Watch a movie (preferably a comedy).
- Read about successful artists and what they did to overcome setbacks.
- Try something new. Fire your agent, switch publishing houses or magazines. Write in a different style and submit it to new markets.

Extra

How to Get Rid Of a Bad Mood

Natalie had had a dreadful day. She'd received three rejections for the same story, gotten an email from her editor saying that they wanted a second rewrite, her computer had crashed and her husband wouldn't be home to help with dinner. She had two options: allow the day to make her miserable or work through her mood. She decided to get rid of her bad mood. You can too. Here's how.

Take a deep breath and, while doing so, tense all your muscles. Hold for a few seconds then release while visualizing all the frustration, annoyance, and anger leaving your body. Now imagine yourself in a place of peace, whether it is in the woods or a jungle. Picture a gentle rain falling, washing all your disappointments and frustrations away.

Remember that the subconscious doesn't differentiate between what is real and what is "made up." Give yourself permission to daydream.

Doubt

*In the hours of adversity be not without hope/
For crystal rain falls from black clouds*
— PERSIAN POEM

*Doubt is a thief that often makes us fear
to tread where we might have won.*
— SHAKESPEARE

Paul checked his mailbox and halted at the sight of the manila envelope with his handwriting scribbled on it. He tossed it on the table and didn't open it. He was tired of rejections. After four years of trying and a drawer full of rejections, he was seriously considering giving up. How much battering could an ego take? It seemed no one but his family liked his writing and even they weren't sure anymore about his ability.

He'd submitted stories to literary magazines, trade journals, even publishing houses and all he'd gotten were form rejections with a "try again" here and there. He started to believe he was no good, that his dream would never come true. He knew he could never write like the best-selling author X. Unfortunately, he also couldn't write in the current popular style that seemed to make new authors rich. Nobody cared whether he wrote again anyway. He was ready to quit.

Months later, Paul finally opened the envelope and inside was a letter from the editor, enthusiastic about his work but asking for a minor revision in order to publish the work. Paul's heart fell. Because of his doubts, he lost a great opportunity.

Many new writers let doubt stop them. The "So What?" question echoes. *If I stop writing, so what? No one will miss it. No one is waiting for my story or article. I don't count.* Yes, you do. Many writers live with doubt. They write thinking that they have no talent, no gift, no skill but they continue to write. Keep writing. Each draft makes you better. Recognize the days before publication as an apprenticeship. You're in training like a musician or a dancer. Even if you have published a few books that haven't done well in the market, consider yourself in training at an advanced level.

Everyone has doubts; having doubts is normal. After writing over 100 books and selling hundreds of millions of copies, Nora Roberts still worries when she sends a manuscript to her editor. If she still has doubts, you can too.

Steps to Handling Doubts

- Read about other writers.
- Repeat an affirmation.
- Read something you wrote that made you proud.

Doubt

- Write your own happy ending.

- Recognize that not everything you write is meant for publication. That poem that cheered up a friend accomplished its purpose. The article that informed your neighbor of the benefits of mulch finished its cycle.

- Offer your services for free. If the market has made you feel useless, use your talents locally. Help promote a fundraiser, write for your community bulletin, write a play for a school, or help create a brochure for a new business. Writers are always needed somewhere.

- Offer your services for a fee. You never know, someone may pay you double what you expect if you ask for it. Give it a try. You may surprise yourself.

Doubt doesn't mean you don't have confidence. Doubt is normal. We all experience it, but you need to replace it with moments of joy.

Effort

What is written without effort is read without pleasure.
SAMUEL JOHNSON

Most people don't like the word effort. That is why "fast and easy" are always used to market things. Many new writers think that writing should be effortless. It should just flow from the mind to the paper. They think desire and talent are all that's needed for a successful career. Desire and talent fill up MFA programs all over the place, yet most of those hopefuls will never be published.

Some will not be published because they refuse to learn grammar, to revise, or to spend the extra time to polish their work; others will not be published because they expect it to be easy. Desire and talent are great nouns, but to survive in this business you need verbs. Effort is what will separate you from the pack.

Expect slow days, grumpiness, frustration, and fear, but continue to make the effort. New writers usually disappear at the stage where an editor suggests a change, or a rejection comes in, or a story isn't working. They throw up their hands, believing others have it easier. Some do, some don't. Don't worry about anyone else, focus on you. Keep in the game and you'll reap your own rewards. Doubt hums a haunting tune even to the most prolific, successful writers, so realize that it's good. It means you want to do a good job and are striving for excellence.

Now!

Suffering is caused by wanting things to be otherwise.
STEPHEN LEVINE

In order to hear your calling and answer it, you must generously give yourself the gift of time. It's not how fast you make your dreams come true, but how steadily you pursue it.
SARAH BAN BREATHNACH

Someone's going to reach the finish line before you do and it's going to hurt. However, writing is a race that never finishes. Remember it is a mission not a goal. One year a certain writer will get his first book or article published. For someone else it may happen months or years down the road. Take your time, it will come, your name will be seen. It's hard wanting validation now, now, now! You want to write faster, sell more, be rich and be famous. NOW! Enjoy the process. It's the only thing you have complete control over. Wanting things now gives others power and then critiques will hurt more and rejections may be fatal. Keep going.

Depression

David is a writer of short stories and articles, but can find no joy in his achievements. He is in a dark place. "I can't write," he says. "I'm always tired. I hate the morning. I sleep all the time, I can't think. I have no energy or ideas and nothing matters to me any more." When sadness turns into something deeper or darker, please seek professional help. The problem may be bigger than you realize and more serious than you can deal with alone. But if you're experiencing a mild case of the blues, it may be a signal that you need time off. Time to be alone and let your spirit rest. Many writers turn to stimulants to get them through: caffeine, alcohol, food or drugs. At first these choices may seem like a nice quick fix, but in the long run, some of these choices have ruined careers and lives.

If You're Feeling the Blahs Try This

- Hide. It's okay to not want to talk to anyone. To spend all day in bed. Pull the curtains because you hate the sight of the sunny day; unplug the phone. Eat what you want to. Read, listen to music, or cry.

- Get a friend to help you with the tasks you're too tired to manage, such as mowing the lawn, washing your hair, washing the dishes or ironing your clothes.

- Staying in a cluttered environment or feeling ugly can compound your depression, so have someone help you clean up. If the lethargy slips into the next day or into a week, please schedule time with a trusted friend or a counselor. It may be something more than the blahs.

- Schedule some down time every week. If you have a habit of feeling down, you may be pushing yourself too hard.

- Daydream about how things will be when you're past this moment.

- Get out.

- Talk to someone.

When it Hurts too Much

Suicide is a frightening reality in this field. Being a writer is a solitary endeavor, and it can be painful. It is one of the most overcrowded arts and you will get little respect. In no other field are beginners expected to be giant successes after the first try.

If you were a new doctor, no one would expect you to become an internationally known specialist after a year of practice. But publish one book, and people will ask you why you didn't make *The New York Times* Bestseller List, sell movie rights, or get a $100,000 advance like the teenager they read about. Ignore them. Guard your joy. If people ask you how much money you make, ask them their salary first then tell them if they're close. Or don't respond at all.

It's okay to be a beginner. It's okay not to make six figures with your first book (or sixth book), or a thousand dollars for your first article. You are on your way.

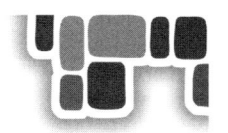

The Ultimate Dream Killer

Everything you need you already have. You are complete right now, you are a whole, total person not an apprentice person on the way to some place else. Your completeness must be understood by you and experienced in your thoughts as your own personal reality.

WAYNE DYER

Argue for your limitations, and sure enough they're yours.

RICHARD BACH

Excuses are one of the biggest dream killers in a writer's life. Something happens and you're knocked flat. Excuses give you a great reason to stay down and never get up again. They are prevalent and insidious, causing a lot of untold stories and ideas to remain so. Why? Because everyone believes them.

I can't write because I don't have time.

I can't write because I'm too old or too young or too hip or not hip enough.

I can't write because I was awful in English or never went to college.

I can't write because I don't think I'm good enough.

I can't write because I have an illness and that makes me tired all the time or I can't see clearly or my arthritis acts up.

There are many excuses, but I'll address the three most common.

I Don't Have Time

Sure you do. You're just not spending it on your dreams. Like money, time is something you spend and many people waste hours. They say they'll wait until their kids are grown, or until they have a better job or until an extra hour is added to each day. The reality is that time will always be taken from you, if you don't know how to steal it. When I was going to college, working full-time and shuttling my mother to and from different doctor appointments, I would write in the waiting rooms, during my lunch break or on the metro. Another writer strapped for time hired a babysitter, another talked into a tape recorder while driving to work. Learn to seize sixty minutes out of every hour or sixty seconds out of every minute. Become a crafty thief of time.

How to Steal Time

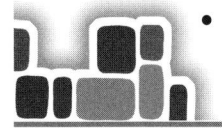

- Make a list of what you do each day. Find one activity that you can farm out or stop doing all together. For example, is there a TV show you must see every day? Why not tape it? Do you commute by bus, metro, or carpool? Write on the way to work or on your lunch break. If you don't take lunch breaks, start.

- Use a tape recorder in the car, while cooking, folding clothes, walking.

- Go to sleep a half hour later or wake up a half hour earlier to write.

- Write in five to fifteen minute intervals. Just to jot down an idea. In the kitchen, while boiling water, scribble down a sentence. *On Sunday, Malcolm discovered the body.* Good you're done for the day. Tomorrow you'll add something more and the day after that even more. It doesn't matter how much you put down, just that you write something. It's like using drops of water to fill a bucket. Eventually, each drop will accumulate into a story. Slowly you'll eke out more time to write.

Don't let time be the enemy of your dreams. Don't dream of the day when you'll have all the time you need to write. Make time now.

I'm Not Smart Enough

Life is my college. May I graduate well and earn some honors!
LOUISA MAY ALCOTT

You are smart enough and don't let anyone tell you otherwise. I doubt my fourth grade teacher would believe I'm a writer now. I missed most of recess that year because I was kept inside to redo my English tests (grammar, spelling etc.), but I still wrote stories and poems and plays. I kept writing. Successful or smart people recognize their limitations and hire others to compensate for them. You have all the skills you need to make your writing dreams come true and one of those skills is delegation.

Use other people's strengths to your advantage. Are you unsure about your subject? Talk to an expert. Grammar not a strong point? Read a book, hire someone, or get a trusted friend to look it over for you. Are you a poor speller? So what. Write the way you think the words are spelled then look them up later or just use spell check on your computer or have someone proofread. The one thing you need to remember is that readers want others to instruct them or to tell them a good story. They don't care about your limitations or shortcoming as long as your words do their job. You're only limited by your fears.

I Have a Disease

I will in no way belittle the burdens of a disease, but don't let it stop you. The writer Christy Brown (the subject of the movie *My Left Foot,* a great inspirational movie) had a major handicap and still made his literary contribution. Debbie Macomber overcame dyslexia to become a *New York Times* Best-Selling writer. Eva Rutland is blind and uses speech recognition. After his near fatal accident, Steven King continued to write through the pain. There are authors who have continued writing after surviving cancer, struggling with muscular dystrophy, dealing with diabetes and coping with many other ailments.

I, too, struggle with a chronic illness that impacts my "quality of life." I faced ten years of being undiagnosed (and at times, misdiagnosed) and I continue to struggle in managing my illness, but my writing kept me going and continues to do so. I don't focus on my illness and I encourage others to do the same. Your words are needed.

Write for five minutes a day. That's all. It will add up.

It's the act of movement that differentiates the winners from the losers. Winners keep moving like the turtle, unlike the hare that finds reasons to stop. Get moving. Toss away excuses, they have no place in your dream plan.

Excuses are easy to fall into and are the enemy of resilience. When you have written only three pages of a three hundred-page novel, the "I don't have time" excuse will pop up. A rejection turns into an "I'm not smart enough" campaign. You see a fresh-faced young writer get a million-dollar contract and you tell yourself that you could have written that book if you weren't always so sick.

Excuses are the perfect shield for fear and the longest and most painful road to regret. You can be yourself (flawed, imperfect) and succeed. Get rid of excuses and take responsibility for your dreams.

I know this section might make some of you angry. Many aspiring writers write me and say, "You don't understand! I have a really good excuse!" You probably do and that's fine. I just hope that it's good enough to combat regret.

After excuses, the next dream killer is the Poverty Complex. Many people think that writers are either very rich or very poor. But there are plenty of writers who are making a good living and you can be one of them. Don't fall into the Poverty Complex. Here are a few tips on how to avoid it.

Make Money Matter

Because the thought of poverty is a dream killer, think of riches. Yes, there are people who will write for free. This fact can make it difficult to earn a living. Don't worry about it. Set your standards and go for high markets. Make sure to work with those who value your skill and will pay for it. Kill the starving artist stereotype. Unless it gives you pleasure, pay no mind to the statement "It's impossible to make a living as a writer." It's a poverty trap. People won't pay for writing if they can get away with it. But don't let them.

As a professional, demand to be paid. If it's a low paying market, make sure you're in it for the right reasons (good exposure, to get clips etc.) but don't stay there. Branch out into bigger markets.

Make money matter. You don't want to live on noodles for the rest of your life and you don't have to. You don't need to be greedy or obnoxious, just business savvy. A check always helps the ego.

Develop the key attitude that you deserve to make a living as a writer: Whether that is through self publishing, charging $100 an hour or demanding an advance of $15,000 or more. Don't fall into the starving artist trap. The world at large will trick you into thinking that you must love what you do at the expense of money. But you have to eat. A person who hands out fries gets paid and so should you.

Book publishers don't make most of their money on books, they make it on selling the rights to those books. You're selling information that can become much more. Synergy is the name of the game: learn how can you take one idea and transform it into different forms.

Audio, scripts, articles, merchandise, try to see the bigger picture *before* you hand over all your rights. Be strategic. If you decide to take a low advance because there are other benefits to the deal, that's strategy. Taking a low advance or low pay because you're grateful someone's willing to pay you, that's a poverty trap.

Getting Started

I've met many individuals who want a career as a writer, but who won't make it because they haven't mastered the first step. They can't get started. They do a lot of busy work, but no writing. This isn't uncommon; it's a safety net. You can't criticize what is not written. You can't be judged on what you haven't done. Unfortunately, dreams can die in the process.

Page fright is a common malady among beginning writers and even among some professionals. It panics writers until they're buried under how-to books, overwhelmed with lecture notes, have watched numerous documentaries, read biographies and done *everything* except what they need to do—write. Similar to experiencing stage fright, you encounter a blank page in all its brilliance and as you stare you feel yourself grow smaller and your ideas grow less significant. You worry about revealing yourself to be a fool, an uncreative fool with no original thoughts or ideas, no ability to add to the millions of works that came before you. You know the first sentence—no the first word—is important, but how can you compete with:

- "Call me Ishmael" (Herman Melville, *Moby Dick*)
- "As Gregor Samsa awoke one morning from uneasy dreams he found himself transformed in his bed into a gigantic insect." (Franz Kafka, *The Metamorphosis*)
- "Jack Torrance thought: officious little prick." (Stephen King, *The Shining*)
- "Death with all its cruel beauty, lived in the bayou." (Nora Roberts, *Midnight Bayou*)

Soon drops of sweat moisten the page or keyboard and you know there's something in the kitchen that needs to be cleaned (the knives look kind of dull).

Halt! Stay where you are. This is not a time to flee; it is a time to fight with words. Any words. Your first try need not be brilliant. Why do you think there are erasers or delete buttons? If you don't have access to either of those, use Wite-out®. Write badly, you're allowed to. No one will see. You don't have any ideas? Try these:

- Write about the stain on your carpet.
- Create an imaginary feature story.
- Write about the next door neighbor's screaming parrot.
- Write about how you sometimes wish your family would disappear.
- Write about a talking pin cushion.
- Rewrite a fairy tale.
- Change the ending of one of your favorite novels or movies.

Getting Started

- Write a letter to an invisible friend.
- Create a diary entry of a crazy afternoon you never had.
- Pretend you're a famous novelist. You receive hundreds of fan letters a day, the critics love you, your editor adores you. The world can't wait for your next book. They don't care what it is as long as it has your name on it. Now get started.
- If that is too far fetched, pretend you're somebody else. Create a different persona. Now write.

Trick your mind in any manner you can think of just so that you can write. Write even as your fingers tremble and your mind tells you (in the voice of all your discouragers) "No, no, no! This is no good. STOP!" Write until the blank page looses its power and is destroyed. Jump into the icy waters of a blank page and write yourself to shore.

Creative Block

Writer's block is only a failure of the ego.

NORMAN MAILER

I don't really believe in *writer's* block, because blocks happen to most artists. Its symptoms are common: sleepless nights, pacing, hair pulling, depression, and crumbled paper. The reason? Fear. Fear of failure, fear of success, fear that an idea is too big or too small, fear that you're unworthy, fear that you have no right to be a writer, fear that you're not a "real" writer, or fear that you may not be the genius you'd thought (or at least hoped) you were. These fears strike all writers at some time in their lives.

Those writers who aren't paralyzed by it learn to pat fear on the head or look at it with amusement as one would regard a child throwing a tantrum. Others face it with white knuckles, determined not to surrender to the monster of doubt. Some cry through it. What they all have in common is the ability to keep writing. They may not continue working on the manuscript that originally brought on the fear, but they work on something, something that will get them through it.

Scared? You're supposed to be. You're baring your soul to a public that might throw tomatoes at you or worse, deem you brilliant at a level you can never live up to. Writing is all that will save you. Keep at it.

Ways to Overcome a Creative Block

- Talk into a tape recorder. Or dictate to a friend.

- Pretend you're one of the characters in your story and write about an average day in your life.

- Write a letter about your problem.

- Come up with other writing projects to work on.
  It usually helps to work on different projects so that when one project stalls you can work on something else.

- Be outrageous. Make something really strange suddenly happen in your story. Like a purple dinosaur being discovered or the hero contemplating a sex change.

- Procrastinate. Listen to music or watch TV. Surround yourself with other artists.

- Use affirmations. You're probably beating yourself up. Stop. Tell yourself positive things. "I'm a great writer and I deserve to succeed." "I serve, the universe provides." "I have limitless ideas." "I am wonderful, talented and creative."

- Take pictures and write about the images.

- Eat a different food or wear something you usually wouldn't. Write about how you feel.

Creative Block

- Take a nap.
- Write about how awful you feel.
- Interview someone local. Most people are willing to share their stories.
- Try to write the most boring story or article you can.
- Bribe yourself. "If you do this then you can do that."
- Read the comics and come up with a different gag or storyline for some of the strips.
- Take a walk.
- Pretend you're a tourist and write about your neighborhood.
- Write a personal ad for the kind of story or idea you're looking for. For example: "Desperate Writer seeking novel idea, preferably of the romantic sort with lots of twists and turns. Any race welcome. Must be long and interesting…" or "Lonely Writer in search of short affair with mystery and danger."
- Write a limerick.
- Play hooky.
- Watch a movie then retell it from a different viewpoint.
- Time yourself. Write something (anything!) for ten minutes. Don't judge it, just get it down and then you're free to spend the rest of the day doing anything you wish.
- Breathe. You'll be okay.

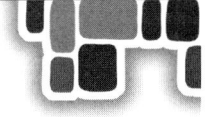

Extra

Sleep On It

I know a writer who, when faced with a creative block, asks herself a question right before going to sleep, and then always wakes up with the answer she needed. I find that it works for me. This is how she does it.

Before going to bed, tell your subconscious your writing problem. After giving it the responsibility to solve the problem, fall asleep and don't think about it. The key is to trust your subconscious to come up with the answer you need. The subconscious never sleeps so it can work on it all night for you. It doesn't have the same censors as the conscious mind, so it will come up with ideas you never thought possible. The benefit is that you won't lose sleep and you will wake up refreshed and ready to go the next day with the solution you need.

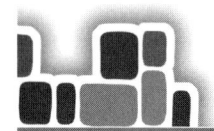

Write Anyway

So now the page is no longer blank; instead it's been vandalized. A perfectly good page wasted by crap. Take a deep breath and keep writing. Not everything you write will smell like roses, sometimes it's just the fertilizer. If you're really having a hard time, take brief breaks. But not for long, otherwise depression may settle in and soon you'll fear you'll never start again.

You don't have to feel smart, special or good enough to write. Write despite your moods. That's what professionals do. Keep going. Spread the crap until something grows.

The Truth about Imagination

You don't have to behave like a child to be creative or to have a mind full of wonder and imagination. I am always annoyed when people offer adults advice that you have to "think like a child" to be artistic, joyful or wonderful. Personally, I have found some children just as closed minded and boring as adults. Ever try to tell a two year old something that they know is not true? Some will become very upset. As an adult you have had varied experiences and you can accept the absurd.

Your mind is powerful. People (children included) create the unusual to fill in parts that need logic. For example, if they wondered why rain falls and didn't know, they would come up with a story about a man who is crying in the sky, which sounds perfectly logical. The ancient Greeks weren't necessarily being imaginative when they created their myths. They were coming up with explanations for then-present mysteries. Still don't believe me? Try telling a religious group that their sacred text is a collection of myths by imaginative storytellers. I suggest you disappear quickly thereafter.

Imagination isn't ignorance. There's a story of a small tribe that planted tin cans because they believed they could grow automobiles. Because they grew everything else they thought this next step was logical. Some people would call this imagination. I would not. Now, if someone who knew that you couldn't grow automobiles out of tin cans came up with the above idea, that would be imaginative to me.

Imagination is knowing the truth and coming up with a different way to look at or perceive something. You are imaginative now. You don't need to jump into mud puddles or play hide and seek unless you want to. You can see the inconceivable. You don't need to be a child or childlike to do so. Those with less education and children at times *do* see or have dazzling insight because they have less of a framework to work from; however, don't let that stop you from seeing things in both a complex and simplistic fashion.

Comparison

*"I will not Reason and Compare.
My business is to create."*

— BLAKE

If you want to kill your confidence faster than a hasty rejection, bad review or degrading critique, compare yourself to others. It doesn't matter if the writer to whom you compare yourself is good or bad, you'll still feel miserable. Why? Because if the writer is bad you'll wonder why they're a bigger success than you are (published, better paid, better looking or, Gasp! younger). If they're good, you'll know why and wonder if you should even attempt to foist your inferior product on the unsuspecting masses. So stop!

Comparison is as useful an activity as pulling out your own teeth. It's painful and you'll look bad. Write, write, write! Keep those blinders on. You're supposed to write because you have something to share and it will be unique because of your voice, your style, and your perceptions. There are no original stories or ideas, just original ways to tell them.

If you're feeling extremely down, take a hiatus from trade magazines. They applaud the chosen few and perpetuate the scarcity mindset, and you'll hate yourself for not being one of the chosen few. Fortunately, you're above that. There is plenty of praise to go around. Comparing will cause you to forget that you are lucky to be a writer. Many others dream to be, but just don't have the courage and they're miserable comparing themselves to YOU.

Integrity

There's a lot of literary prostitution in the arts. Many writers sell their wares only for the money. I'm not against the practice, I've seen it make people rich, but I've also seen it destroy souls.

If you can keep one thing, keep your integrity. Always do your best. Don't be seduced into changing your voice or your style for money. This is not obstinacy, this is preservation. You must find the editor who gets your voice, because some won't. You want to be proud of your work no matter how small. Some writers change articles or stories to suit an editor, then when the editor still hates the work the writer is left with a dead piece.

People read to be entertained or informed. Do your best to meet those needs.

If you want to freelance, choose an area that you know about or that interests you. Who cares if at the time health writers are making a killing? If you know a lot about gardening, then this is a lucrative field for you. Become the best at what you do.

Comparison

Genre fiction make you cringe? Then don't write it! Don't let the marketplace dictate your work. Write only what you can write. That's the path to success and brilliance.

Envy

Of course, there will be times when you just can't help yourself and you will compare. That's when it will strike: A festering disease of the spirit. You'll feel embarrassed and disgusted with yourself and with the person who has made you feel this way (basically yourself, again). Envy. It's perfectly normal. Don't ignore it. Own your emotions; ignoring them will only make you feel worse. I hate it when someone suffers a particularly bad blow (fired, dumped, hurt) and her (purported) friend pats her on the back and coos a silly platitude. "Sorry your dreams are now in ashes, love. *Don't feel bad.*" What the #@$!? What planet do you live on? I feel awful! Angry, pissed and plenty of other things. We are writers after all, and our rantings can be long and fierce. But that's what writers do for a living—feel. We feel everything, intensely, so when envy creeps up on us or grabs us in a chokehold, it lingers and rages. See it, feel it. However, some writers invite it to dinner and allow it to destroy their lives. I don't recommend that.

How to Handle Envy

- Write a story of someone envying you.
- Sulk for a day (it's allowed).
- Give praise. You don't have to be sincere.
- Admit it. If someone tells you about their good fortune say "I'm so envious."
- Give gifts (making someone else feel better can help make you feel better. You won't feel like such a jerk).
- Have a tantrum. No one needs to see.
- Read about top authors envying each other.
- Remember when you succeeded at something and treasure that time.
- Buy yourself something.
- Get writing so that you can write something that will have people envying you.

Sometimes envy sheds a light on what we want. Annoyed with the actor who has written a children's book? Write one yourself. Jealous of the friend with a great agent? Change your agent, or list the qualities you want in your relationship with your agent and aim for that.

If you envy someone for being younger, prettier, taller or anything else you can't possibly achieve, write about it. Make a spoof of it. You may as well use your emotions for your art.

Still steaming because someone has what you want? Here's a little tale to help you. Remember being a kid and seeing the ice cream truck come around the corner? You try to rush to the front of the line so that your order will be first, but another kid gets there first. Before you lunge for the kid's throat, a wise guardian gently holds you back and says, "Wait your turn." Do that.

Creative Flood

> Do not confuse motion and progress.
> A rocking horse keeps moving but does not
> make any progress.
>
> ALFRED A. MONTAPERT

The opposite of a creative block is a creative flood, and it can be just as damaging to the writer's life. In this state, your mind is full of ideas and, at first, it seems like an abundance of riches. I'm not referring to writing flow (when time escapes you and the words spill forth), I'm talking about when words and ideas drown you. When you can't focus on anything. When you have fifteen story ideas, twenty poems, five publishers you want to query, eighteen magazines you wish to write for, you're designing a new writing space, and have identified sixteen agents you want to contact.

A creative flood is when you start many projects that overwhelm you. This is another example of fear. Having too much to do can paralyze you. Too many story ideas may cause you never to finish one.

> *I went for years not finishing anything. Because of course, when you finish something you can be judged...I had poems which were re-written so many times I suspect it was just a way of avoiding sending them out.*
>
> ERICA JONG

Creative flood or overproduction can be another word for perfectionism. Being busy is important and so is creativity, but when it stops you, it's a burden. When working on one idea, it's okay for you to jot down another that comes to mind, but don't abandon one project for another unless it is a calculated move.

Steps to Overcoming the Creative Flood

- Recognize when it happens so you can act accordingly. Creative floods can cause writing "burn out" so monitor how you're feeling.

- Always carry a notebook with you to jot down ideas.

- Create small steps. It is possible to learn three languages, paint, play an instrument, write three poems, two letters and a novel but not in one day. Make each step manageable.

- If you have many things that you wish to accomplish in one day, create a loose schedule. It can mimic the ones you had in school. Say 7:30 music, 8:00 poetry.

- Run, jump rope, dance. Exercise can use up the extra energy you have and may help you to think clearly.

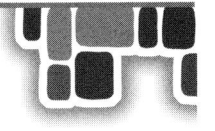

- Select a friend to help you come up with a strategy so you won't become overwhelmed. Or create an SOS signal when you are close to experiencing a flood.

- Take five minute breaks. Do something toward your goal in five minute increments. Paint some, write some, or organize some, all in five minute segments.

Also remember that there are times when you will need to keep still to hear your inner voice tell you what steps you need to take next.

Success

If your success is not on your own terms, if it looks good to the world, but does not feel good in your heart, it is not success at all.

ANNA QUINDLEN

We all work towards success, yet most people don't know how to handle the onslaught of good fortune when it comes. The sudden adulation, money, and status can become another stress for which one may be unprepared.

Suddenly, you're no longer a person writing in solitude, you're besieged by a public that feels that they now own you. You will be subject to criticisms, spoofs, and gossip. People will demand more work, time and energy from you. If you're not careful, you may burn out. So you need to be aware of the hazards of success:

- Lost time. People will want you. They will request that you give speeches, interviews, and workshops. They will ask that you participate in fundraisers, judge contests or teach.
- Your phone will start ringing with a regularity you never thought possible.
- If you reach a bestseller list, you will be pressured to stay on the list or hit a higher slot.
- Your objectivity could change. Some writers who reach success start to believe their press and soon they become crazy with the belief that they are the "next best thing" and turn into a giant ego.
- Your core values may be influenced. Thought you'd never become a diva? When you have people hanging on your every word and have loads of disposable income it may be easy to arrive late to dinners or talk about yourself at every occasion.
- Friends or family members may become jealous of you.
- Family members or friends may accuse you of using them as characters in your work.
- Other writers may accuse you of stealing their ideas.
- You may have to travel to twenty-one cities in two weeks.

But you don't have to be a victim of success. All you need to do is learn to manage it in whatever form it comes to you.

Ways to Handle Success

- Take a break and reflect. It's okay to go on a vacation right after a book makes a big splash or after an article causes a huge controversy.
- Know your allies. You will likely lose some friends who will be envious of your

success, but treasure those who stick by you and be aware that you will make new ones.

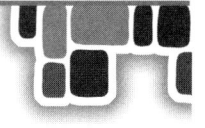

- Remember your mission statement. It is easy to get caught up in what others believe is "being a success." Whether that is partying, traveling, interviewing or the like.

- Mind your tongue. Don't put down those who haven't reached your level. It always amazes me how many published authors become snobs against the unpublished.

- Get an unlisted number. If too many people are calling you, don't be readily available.

- Learn to say "no." Many people will want your time, and initially you will want to please them all. You can't, so don't try.

- Hire help. Get someone to handle your correspondence or someone to help you with household chores. Hire an assistant to help you with the details.

- Meet others in the field to talk about strategies and tactics for handling success.

- Get a good, trustworthy and reputable business manager. Many writers are not good business people and lose money quickly. Unless you have a trusted friend or family member who is good in business, do your research and hire someone who can help you with taxes, contracts, and other business and financial matters. You don't want the government or a lawsuit at your door.

Your success may take time away from your family. In that instance, have a discussion with them so that everyone can learn to adjust to your newfound popularity.

Remember that success is not a destination; so be gracious when you pass it by. You'll always want more. One bestseller will lead to the desire for a second bestseller. One huge check will create the desire for a larger check. Keep your goals and mission in order. Don't let the thrill of success become a drug.

Part Three
Four Steps to Resilience

Get Support

You can't survive the creative life alone. You need a person or group to help you get through the rough patches. Successful writers use agents to help guide their careers, are part of a writing or critique group, belong to an organization(s) or rely on a family member for support. Oprah has a production team; Stephen King has his wife. Who can you turn to when times are tough? Try to build your support network.

- Find a mentor. A mentor doesn't necessarily have to be in the writing field. Find someone who is living her dream and is willing to listen to you and can offer you advice and encouragement.

- Join a group. Local or national. Become part of a writing group online or offline. Be around other writers who are happy being writers (it's easy to slip into groups that just complain about the writing industry, and that's not good for you).

- Volunteer with a writing organization. This will help you to get out and about. Far too many writers isolate themselves.
- Share. Tell a trusted friend or family member about your intention.
- Get inspiration. Get the life stories of three people you admire (whether it is a book, movie or audio) and make them available whenever you feel down.
- Attend writing courses or conferences. It helps to be around people of like minds.

Extra

Focus Your Revenge

Those of you who believe in forgiving people who have mistreated you, please skip this suggestion. You won't need it. For those of you with a little wickedness, please consider the following:

Think of someone who mocked you, a bully in school who shoved you into lockers or a girl who always made fun of your clothes, a boss who wouldn't get off your back, an ex- who said you'd never amount to anything, or a parent or teacher who belittled you. Put that person(s) firmly in your mind then write to show them how wrong they were (are). Develop your career so that it can become an eloquent F—you.

It's okay to write out of vengeance. Sometimes you won't find a community or buddy that suits you. Use this as your support instead. It is okay to follow your dreams just to prove all your naysayers wrong. Become a big success; that is the best revenge.

Relax

*A writer's life should be a tranquil life.
Read a lot and go to the movies.*

MARIO PUZO

Self-care is critical for resilience. The world will not come to an end if you don't write for a few days, or format a manuscript incorrectly, or realize your 400-page novel is a pile of garbage. There will be days or moments when you won't feel like doing anything. You'll want to curl up in your bed and hide from the world. That's fine, you're still a writer. It's not whether you stop writing; it's for how long.

A couple of days is okay, but a couple of months or years? Well, then something else is going on and you need to face it.

- Remember to exercise. It helps the blood to pump and your body will be better able to fight off disease and the effects of disappointment. It also helps keep your brain healthy.

- Eat fruits and vegetables. The right diet can help you maintain energy and overall good health. The foods below can help fight fatigue, improve the appearance of your skin and help with stamina. Carbohydrates (protein, dairy and fruits and vegetables) are great energy boosters. Consider eating:

Fruit yogurt

Toast with beans, cheese, or peanut butter

Fruit salad

Fruit juices or smoothies

Dried fruit (dried apricots are a great source of fiber and iron which prevents tiredness)

Bananas

Nuts

Be creative. Grab a cookbook of power foods and incorporate them into your diet.

- Refill the well. Don't forget that it is your job to be in touch with art. Visit museums, theaters, sports events, movies, restaurants or whatever gives you joy. Remember to be alive. You can't write about life if you can't live it fully. Watch a cartoon, a funny movie, read the comics have a good laugh. *Read.* Many writers stop reading for some reason. Some say they don't have time, others that they don't want to know what "the competition" is up to. Read. Fill the well. Applaud a good story or well written article. They are not your competitors, they are your sisters and brothers and teachers and friends. Learn to safely love another's work without putting your own work down. You're not a good judge anyway. Enjoy the pleasure of someone celebrating life.

Relax

"If you stuff yourself full of poems, essays, plays, stories, novels, films, comic strips, magazines, music, you automatically explode every morning like Old Faithful. I have never had a dry spell in my life, mainly because I feed myself well, to the point of bursting."
— RAY BRADBURY

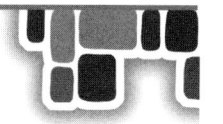

- Prepare for success. At some time each day give yourself a pep talk. Many successful people have a mantra or affirmation that they repeat to themselves. Some salespeople give themselves talks to get the courage they need to sell their products. Start your day with this statement or a variation:

"I'm a talented author with many readers eager for my stories or articles. I am an asset to my publishing company (magazine, client) and make more money than I could ever need. I have all the skills I need to succeed at my goal."

This exercise helps to trick your mind so you'll face the day with eagerness and confidence.

- Create a safe haven. It is important that you create a safe haven, a place where you can retreat and be your authentic self. A place where all the labels (mother, sister, husband, dad, dentist, Asian, HIV positive) are erased and you are who you truly are. This safe haven needs to be a place where you can play peaceful music or hard rock; a place to rant, rave, or cry. A place totally yours for however long you want it. It doesn't need to be a sacred place. It can be your bathroom. You can turn it into a safe haven by lighting candles or wearing a certain robe. It can be your closet, your car, or a special location in a park. Any place where you can have a moment of time to get in touch with your feelings. If you need to, save some money and go to a hotel/motel once in a while for a night or two of peace.

- Remember that everything has a season. In your career, you will have a winter season when nothing seems to grow, and the land is barren and cold. You'll look at someone in her bright, fruitful spring season and feel your career is over. It's not. Keep sowing the seeds (creating, sending out, reading) and eventually what you plant will grow.

- Life doesn't always make sense. Remember that bad things happen. Sometimes things happen for no reason. We like to have a logical equation for everything. If you write a brilliant novel, an editor will buy it. If you send out a perfect query, an agent will ask to see more. But that is not always the case. Sometimes the editor is at the wrong publishing house, so that even if they like your work, it's not right for the publisher. Or your article is ahead of its time.

Sometimes there is no reasonable explanation. Not everything that happens will have anything to do with whether you are a kind and generous person. A jerk will get a great book contract, a badly written book will become a bestseller and you won't understand why. It's not your job to make sense of it, just keep doing what you do.

Know Your Limitations

What one has to do usually can be done.

ELEANOR ROOSEVELT

Find out your limitations. This is not a reason to pull out your old list of excuses, but rather a way to face your present situation. Be realistic about the feasibility of your dreams. If you're the main breadwinner with three children under the age of five, it may not be feasible for you to quit your job and write full-time. Your limitations are different from those of a single person with a healthy savings account who can manage to take such a risk. There will be plenty of unknowns out there, try to anticipate the ones that you can readily overcome and acknowledge them early-on.

The Writer Behind the Words

- What kind of writer are you? Do you want to entertain or inform or both? Consider fiction or non-fiction or a mixture.
- Do you like to research? If not, hire a research assistant.
- Do you edit well? If not, hire an editor.
- Do you know how to structure a book? If not, hire a writing coach.
- Do you like to work alone? If not, work with a collaborator.
- Do you type well? If not, hire a typist or dictate.
- Are you patient? If not, try writing short stories, articles and poems instead of a novel.
- Do you want to make money? If not, write for self-actualization not the market. If you do, identify markets that *pay* (you would be amazed by how many writers, write for nothing except to see their name in print, and then complain about not making money. If you can get a hundred dollars or more for your work, go for it).
- Not prolific? Get paid more for each project or find other ways to earn income.
- Not organized? Write by instinct instead of according to a strict schedule.
- Do you enjoy the physical act of writing? If not, consider an alternative.
- Do you have ideas or stories that may shock or embarrass you or others? Use a pen name.
- What are your time constraints?
- Do you like to promote or do you prefer privacy?
- Can you work on many different projects or can you only focus on one at a time? Uncover your limitations so they won't become stumbling blocks in the future.

Extra

New Directions

Changing your mind isn't failure. Failure is stopping in the middle of the race, staring longingly at the finish line but making no move towards it. Changing your mind is stopping in the middle of the race, staring at the finish line, deciding that it's not where you want to go, and switching your direction.

If you decide that writing is not for you and you want to do something else, that is perfectly healthy. My mother started off as a medical illustrator, then realized she wasn't a desk artist and chose a different field. Initially I studied to be a speech pathologist, then realized I didn't have the temperament. One writer started out writing cozy mysteries, then realized she preferred fantasy. Honor your spiritual needs. Perhaps your desire to write is really a desire to communicate. You could consider becoming a public speaker, an oral storyteller, an actor, painter, teacher or counselor.

A writer is someone who *must* write. Writing nourishes them and fills them with ecstasy, not with hours of agony and despair. It's okay to be terrified at times and jubilant at others. Writing doesn't always have to be fun, but if you couldn't imagine doing anything else then you're following your bliss.

As life moves on, your desires may shift and change. Don't lock yourself into a dream just because you had it. Make your dreams suit you, not the other way around.

Get a Strategy

Many writers expect their careers to just happen. They have no plan for how they expect things to move forward. I am not saying that you need to come up with a formal, written business plan. But remember that publishing is a business that has its ups and downs. Here are ways to deal with it.

- Learn to respond rather than react. There are different ways to achieve a goal. The power of choice is our greatest gift as humans. How you chose to respond to a setback will dictate your future—choice is a big responsibility. You can choose to react instinctively or to take a step back and respond consciously.

Consider these two scenarios.

A book comes back rejected for the fifth time. A *reaction* to this would be: My agent is useless, the editors don't understand. They are probably twenty-something MBAs who don't know the first thing about writing. They wouldn't know a good story if it bit them on the bum!

A *response* would be: Damn. I guess X-publisher isn't the right place for me. Perhaps I could shorten the novel to a novella or submit an excerpt to a magazine.

When you react you are ruled by your subconscious and become a slave to your emotions. You will likely mirror habitual behaviors and have your future reflect your past—nothing will change. By responding to a situation, you use your conscious mind to help you achieve desired results. Learn to respond and not react, and take control of your destiny.

- Ask the right questions. People want the world to make sense. They like equations, cause-and-effect. If you do this, then this happens. If something good happens, then most people readily take credit for it. If something bad happens, they try to find someone or something to blame. Sometimes there is no rhyme or reason for a bad event. Sometimes a well-written novel just doesn't sell well, an agent says something abusive, or an editor kills a story with no explanation. Wondering and wallowing will not move you forward. Learn to ask the right questions. Not "Why is this happening to me?" But "What do I do next?" Don't be life's victim.

- Model success. Find a writer with a career you admire in a field that you enjoy. Preferably someone who is still alive, because the publishing industry has changed so dramatically in the past years. Attempt to emulate the strategies used in your favorite writer's career when they hit it big. If they wrote small unremarkable category romances for many years, then broke out with a sweeping saga, then emulate the sweeping saga. (Why suffer more than you need to?)

- Gather industry news in small doses. Don't gather so much information that it depresses you, but know what the atmos-

Get A Strategy

phere is like. Some writers will claim that ignorance is bliss and that, had they known all the trouble out there, they wouldn't have become published. Good for them. But sometimes not knowing what is out there can harm you. There is an unhealthy myth that once you're published it's easy to get an agent, so many published authors despair when an agent turns them down. The truth is that it's always difficult to get an agent. Some authors publish five books before catching the interest of one agent. Others do without agents and hire a literary attorney. Be careful of myths that make you feel as though you're doing something wrong.

- Learn to be flexible. It's good to build up a brand name, but learn to do other things well just in case your chosen arena hits a down market.

- Work towards your mission statement. Do something every day to make it real.

- Brainstorm alternatives. If the current market isn't ready for your voice, consider self-publishing (but do your homework, there are a lot of scam artists out there). Write a blog. Create your own newsletter or magazine. Develop a series of greeting cards or booklets. Offer your services to local companies or community centers. Think outside the box.

- Always write the best that you can. If your book, poem, or article delivers, then you will be asked to do more work and that's what a writer's life is about.

Success is Your Birthright

Successful writers are not the ones who write the best sentences. They are the ones who keep writing. They are the ones who discover what is most important and strangest and most pleasurable in themselves, and keep believing in the value of their work, despite the difficulties.

BONNIE FRIEDMAN

The secret to resilience lies in three words: Faith in movement. To succeed you must always go forward—whether it is a few baby steps or a giant leap—*believing* you are achieving your dream. Write, despite the heartbreaks.

Submit, despite the discouragement. Dream big, despite your present realities. You are on a hallowed path taken by people before you, many of whom are living a life that others are too scared to aim for. You are greater than your circumstance. *Success is yours to claim.*

When you move forward in the faith and belief that wondrous things will happen, they do. You'll draw the right people into your life, a person might need an article or someone knows of a new agent. Money will show up at unexpected moments. Opportunities will appear, don't question them or try to analyze why. Luck is created. Throw away the myth of the chosen few; that mindset is for people who want to struggle in a dog eat dog world. You're above that.

Your desire is proof that you've been chosen to succeed on this path and the universe can't help but make things happen. Don't accept being little and insignificant. If you're meant to be big, then move towards that and positive things will happen.

Life makes sense when you know your purpose. When you no longer feel helpless and useless, every part of your life can be used in your craft, every experience good or bad enriches it.

Losing a contract, an agent, an assignment will no longer be devastating, because you know everything is working to your good. If you lose a contest, just think: "I'm made for bigger and better things."

Learn to let go of the outcome. Once you've written something and edited it, send it out and begin working on something else. Do not attach your hopes, aspirations or expectations to it ("This work will make me rich, it will make me famous." etc.). You can't control trends or the response of people, and if they're not favorable you may wrongly blame your work.

Be of service. Successful writers are aware of their duty, which is to serve a public eager for knowledge, comfort, entertainment or experience. This doesn't mean you become a slave to public opinion, just that you remain aware that you write, not just for your own selfish desires but to provide your words as a gift.

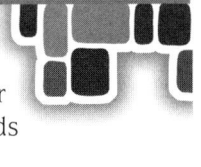

Publishing is a highly competitive field—status, prestige, awards and money are the measuring sticks shoved in the face of anyone who enters the field. Therefore, my statements may sound foolhardy. You'll be bombarded by people who say you must be aggressive, you must promote your books at all times or you'll disappear, you have to run a website, be online, do book signings and interviews etc.

However, I don't believe in anything that takes you away from the most important aspect of being an author/writer: Creating products that people can use. If the internet or book tours or any other activity take you away from creating, then readjust your schedule. You don't have to follow anyone else's lifestyle to be a success.

I was unable to aggressively promote my first two titles: First because that's not my personality and second because in that time span my father was diagnosed with cancer and after that my mother had major surgery. I spent those years in doctor's offices, surgical waiting rooms and hospital suites. I did what I could to promote my books, but I spent my energy taking care of my parents, and writing articles and books. I didn't let the "white noise" of the outside world take away the peace and power of creation. And the universe was kind, my books sold well (though slowly) and my publisher offered me a new contract and continues to do so.

The competitive mindset leads to unhappiness because it feeds on the scarcity mentality that there's not enough to go around. Which, by now, I hope you know is false.

There are many books that outsell books that reach the *New York Times* Bestseller list but that are under the radar of bookstores. Books that make the lists we admire are measured by velocity, not necessarily by quantity. Therefore, a book that sells 50,000 copies in a week will make the list, but a book that slowly sells a million copies in a year won't. Does the writer care? Would you? You're still rich and selling.

There are many paths to success and success is yours to claim. Believe that truth and it will come true. I trust that you will create your own stories of resilience and I welcome you to share them with me.

In the meantime, be kind to the writer behind the words.

And it does no harm to repeat, as often as you can, 'Without me the literary industry would not exist: the publishers, the agents, the sub-agents, the sub-sub agents, the accountants, the libel lawyers, the departments of literature, the professors, the theses, the books of criticisms, the reviewers, the book pages—all the vast and proliferating edifice is because of this small, patronized, put-down and underpaid person'.

DORIS LESSING

Recommended Resources

These books have helped me through hard times and expand on some of the tips I have included in this book. I hope they will help you on your journey.

Books

Make Your Creative Dreams Real: A Plan for Procrastinators, Perfectionists, Busy People, and People Who Would Really Rather Sleep All Day
by SARK (Susan Ariel Rainbow Kennedy)
FIRESIDE, 2004

Making a Literary Life: Advice for Writers and Other Dreamers
by Carolyn See
RANDOM HOUSE, 2002

The Writer Behind the Words

When Bad Things Happen to Good People
by Harold S. Kushner
AVON BOOKS, 1981

Creative Visualization: Use the Power of Your Imagination to Create What You Want in Your Life
by Shakti Gawain
NEW WORLD LIBRARY, 2002

The Courage to Write: How Writers Transcend Fear
by Ralph Keyes
HENRY HOLT AND COMPANY, LLC., 1995

Writing from the Inside Out: Transforming Your Psychological Blocks to Release the Writer Within
by Dennis Palumbo
JOHN WILEY & SONS, INC., 2000

The Artist's Way; A Spiritual Path to Higher Creativity
by Julia Cameron
JEREMY P. TARCHER/PUTNAM, 2002

Zen in the Art of Writing
by Ray Bradbury
BANTAM/CAPRA PRESS, 1992

Beyond the Words: The Three Untapped Sources of Creative Fulfillment for Writers
by Bonni Goldberg
JEREMY P. TARCHER/PUTNAM, 2002

How to Think Like Leonardo Da Vinci: Seven Steps to Genius Every Day
by Michael J. Gelb
DELL PUBLISHING, 1998

Recommended Resources

The Resilient Writer:
Tales of Rejection and Triumph from
23 Top Authors
by Catherine Wald
PERSEA BOOKS, INC., 2005

Writing Down the Bones
by Natalie Goldberg
SHAMBHALA PUBLICATIONS, INC., 1986

Make Your Mind Work for You: New Mind Power Techniques
to Improve Memory, Beat Procrastination, Increase Energy,
and More
by Joan Minninger, Ph.D. and Eleanor Dugan
RODALE PRESS, 1988

The Career Novelist: A Literary Agent Offers Strategies
for Success
by Donald Maass
HEINEMANN, 1996

Superfoods Rx: Fourteen Foods that Will Change Your Life
by Steven G. Pratt, M.D. and Kathy Matthews
HARPERCOLLINS PUBLISHERS, INC., 2004

The Writer's Book of Hope: Getting from Frustration
to Publication
by Ralph Keyes
HENRY HOLT AND COMPANY, LLC, 2003

How to Get Happily Published: A Complete and Candid Guide
by Judith Appelbaum
HARPERCOLLINS PUBLISHERS, 1998

Self-Publishing Manual: How to Write, Print and Sell Your
Own Book by Dan Poynter
PARA PUBLISHING, 2006

The Well-Fed Writer: Financial Self-Sufficiency as a Freelance Writer in Six Months or Less
by Peter Bowerman
FANOVE PUBLISHING, 2000

Good to Great
by Jim Collins
COLLINS, 2001

Organizations

The Academy of American Poets
584 Broadway, Ste. 1208, New York 10012
www.poets.org

The Association of Writers and Writing Programs (AWP)
George Mason University, MSN 1E3, Fairfax, VA 22030
www.awpwriter.org

American Society of Journalists & Authors (ASJA)
1501 Broadway, Ste. 302, New York, NY 10036
www.asja.org

Authors Guild
31 E. 28th St., Fl 10, New York, NY 10016
www.authorsguild.org

Horror Writers Association (HWA)
PO Box 50577, Palo Alto, CA 94303
www.horror.org

Mystery Writers of America (MWA)
17 East 47th St., 6th Floor, New York, NY 10017
www.mysterywriters.org

National Writers Association
10940 S. Parker Rd., #508, Parker, CO 80134
www.nationalwriters.com

National Writers Union (NWU)
113 University Place, 6th Floor, New York, NY 10003-4527
www.nwu.org

Poets & Writers
72 Spring St., New York, NY 10012
www.pw.org

Romance Writers of America (RWA)
16000 Stuebner Airline Road, Ste. 140 Spring, TX 77379
www.rwanational.com

Science Fiction & Fantasy Writers of America (SFWA)
PO Box 171, Unity, ME 04988-0171
www.sfwa.org

Society of Children's Book Writers & Illustrators (SCBWI)
8271 Beverly Blvd., Los Angeles, CA 90048
www.scbwi.org

Organizations

Sisters in Crime
PO Box 442124
Lawrence, KS 66044
www.sistersincrime.org

Society of Children's Book Writers & Illustrators
8271 Beverly Blvd., Los Angeles, CA 90048
www.scbwi.org

A Writer's Prayer

God grant me the courage
to toss the stories I cannot change,
The genius to change the ones I can,
And the humility to know
the difference.

© Dara Girard

About the Author

Dara Girard is an award-winning, multi-published author of fiction and nonfiction. She has written numerous articles for *Byline* magazine, *The Writer's Notebook*, newsletters and e-zines. Ms. Girard is a member of Novelists Inc. and the Published Authors Network. Along with writing articles, Ms. Girard speaks to groups and organizations. Visit her website at www.daragirard.com. You can contact her online or at:

ILORI Press
c/o Dara Girard
PO Box 10332
Silver Spring, MD 20914